Color Made Easy

scrapbooking · cardmaking · papercrafting

Misti Tracy

Bluegrass PUBLISHING

w w w . t h e u l t i m a t e w o r d . c o m
2 7 0 · 2 5 1 · 3 6 0 0

Color Made Easy, published by Bluegrass Publishing, Inc.

For information write:
Bluegrass Publishing, Inc.
PO Box 634
Mayfield, KY 42066 USA
service@theultimateword.com
www.BluegrassPublishing.com

ISBN: 1-59978-007-0

Created by Teeter Bugs™
www.TeeterBugs.com
Creative Director, Designer . Misti Tracy
Associate Art Directors . Lynda Tracy and Kevin Tracy
Contributing Artist . Michelle Johnson

Proudly printed in the United States of America

Dedication

some people come into our lives
make footprints on our hearts
and we are never the same

In Memory of my Grandmother

Naomi Todhunter Booth

who gave me unconditional encouragement

when I needed it most.

I want to thank my Heavenly Father for His continual inspiration in writing this book. I encountered many obstacles which seemed impossible to overcome, but with His help solutions to problems were found.

Through His inspiration I was privileged to meet Linda LaTourelle and Shanda Purcell of Bluegrass Publishing. Without them this book would not be possible, and I thank them for helping make my dream come true! I know miracles happen in our lives when we trust in God.

My family is awesome! I want them to know how much I appreciate them. I'm grateful to my grandfather, James Booth, for his enthusiastic spirit of encouragement and his willingness to give of himself. I'm also grateful to my brother, Ren, for his complete confidence in me to accomplish my goals. My sister, Michelle, and her husband, Aaron, have been my angels! Their generous support has allowed me to complete this book and I thank them from the bottom of my heart. My beautiful niece, Autumn, has brought sunshine into my life especially on my cloudy days! And finally, I'm so grateful to my parents, Kevin and Lynda, for giving me the vision to follow my dreams and for being there when I needed them—a gift I will always treasure.

Love, Misti

Table of Contents

Introduction

Color is everywhere, yet it can be difficult to select just the right palettes for your crafting projects. A color wheel can help, but even that can be confusing.

Now, with *Color Made Easy's* simple, ready-to-use color palettes the work is done for you! Whether you're a beginner or a seasoned pro, it doesn't matter. *Color Made Easy* is great for anyone at any skill level. It's a life-saver for papercrafters who don't want to deal with the frustration of choosing colors. It will save you time by eliminating the guesswork. Plus, those intimidating racks of papers don't stand a chance because you'll be armed with your *Color Buddy*, a great, time-saving tool for selecting paper and embellishments at home or at the store.

It couldn't be easier!

In the pages that follow you'll find endless inspiration to take the guesswork out of choosing colors. Each color palette consists of five expertly coordinated colors, which are broken down into combinations of three colors: dominant, secondary and accent (figure A). You can use any value of these colors depending

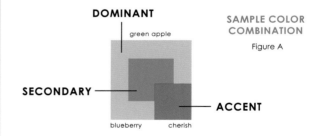

DOMINANT
green apple

SAMPLE COLOR COMBINATION
Figure A

SECONDARY

ACCENT

blueberry   cherish

on the effect you would like to achieve. Use darker colors to add drama and lighter colors to increase subtlety.

There's no need to worry about matching colors to photographs, it's much more important to communicate your theme. This puts more emphasis on your photographs and allows them to stand out.

Want more variety? Create interest by adding a neutral color. The darker the neutral color the more contrast it will create. I've used two neutral colors, jet black and white, in many of my color combinations. Try creating your own look by adding any of the five neutrals: Jet Black, White, Vanilla Bean, Morning Mist, and Decadence.

Stuck in a rut? Use the *Creative Kick-Starts* for each color palette to get your creative juices flowing. You'll find great inspiration for color, design and journaling. Sometimes all we need is a little push!

So, it's as easy as one, two, three! Choose a theme from the *Index of Themes*, select a color combination and...

Start Creating!

Value

lightness and darkness of a color

Neutral

| jet black |
| white |
| vanilla bean |
| morning mist |
| decadence |

Index of Themes

Hot and Trendy

make a *splash* in the *world!*

exciting

active

dramatic

bright

friendly

energy

happy

joyful

fun

electric

cheerful

dynamic

grape fizz

electric lime

sunflower

razzle berry

raindrop

Oh So Sweet

Dominant Color grape fizz
Secondary Color sunflower
Accent Color razzle berry

materials Cardstock (WorldWin) • Patterned Paper (Die Cuts With A View) • Brad (Making Memories) • Ribbon

All play and no work is cool!

Color It! Color Combinations

grape fizz
electric lime   razzle berry

jet black
razzle berry   electric lime

razzle berry
electric lime   sunflower

electric lime
grape fizz   raindrop

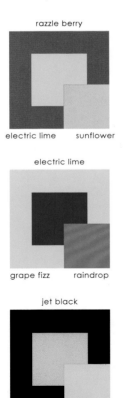

jet black
sunflower   electric lime

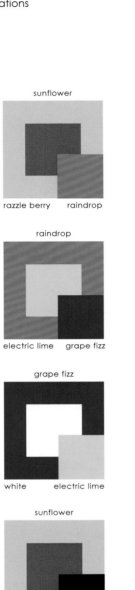

sunflower
razzle berry   raindrop

raindrop
electric lime   grape fizz

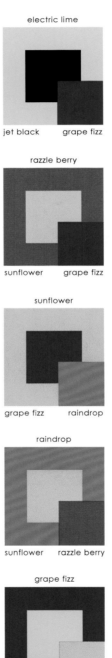

grape fizz
white   electric lime

sunflower
razzle berry   jet black

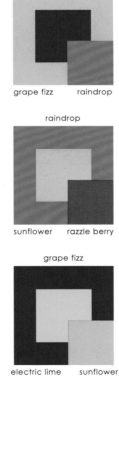

razzle berry
white   grape fizz

electric lime
jet black   grape fizz

razzle berry
sunflower   grape fizz

sunflower
grape fizz   raindrop

raindrop
sunflower   razzle berry

grape fizz
electric lime   sunflower

Create It!

Birthday Party

New Year's Eve

Teens

Youth

School Play

Movie Night

Summer Days

Best Friends

Fashion

Until further notice, celebrate everything!

Happy Birthday!

Dominant Color electric lime
Secondary Color razzle berry
Accent Color sunflower

materials Patterned Paper (Die Cuts With A View) • Ink • Ribbon

Movie Night

Dominant Color raindrop
Secondary Color razzle berry
Accent Color sunflower

materials Cardstock (WorldWin) Patterned Paper (Die Cuts With A View) • Ink • Ribbon

Creative Kick-Starts!

Color
Go window shopping and take note of the color schemes used in new fashions. Also look at the promotional items used to sell the new styles, you may find ideas for trendy type designs.

Journaling
Complete this sentence: My favorite rock-n-roll song of all time is... (write out the lyrics in your own handwriting).

Design
Pick up your favorite trendsetting magazine and scan articles, advertisements, and photos. Look for repeating color schemes, words, catchy phrases and unique layouts.

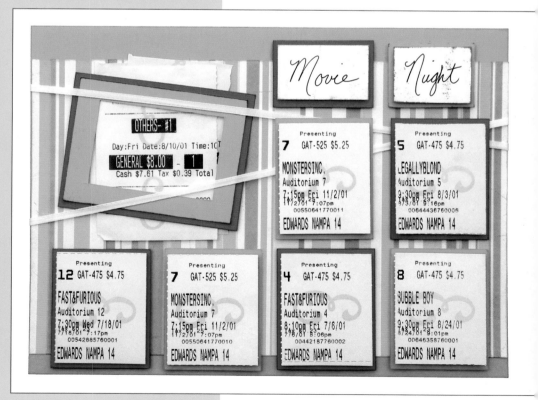

Eclectic

just when my *life*
needed a *touch of color*
you added a *whole rainbow*

youthful
splendid
original
subtle
friendly
distinctive
unique
personality
surprising
playful
unexpected
diverse

cherish

green apple

rose petal

blueberry

apricot

"Rabid Dogs"

Dominant Color cherish
Secondary Color green apple
Accent Colors blueberry
and jet black

materials Eyelets (Making Memories)
Patterned Paper, Sticker (Arctic Frog)
Cardstock · Ink · Hemp

*Life is a great big canvas,
and you should throw all the
paint on it you can.*

—Danny Kaye

Color It! Color Combinations

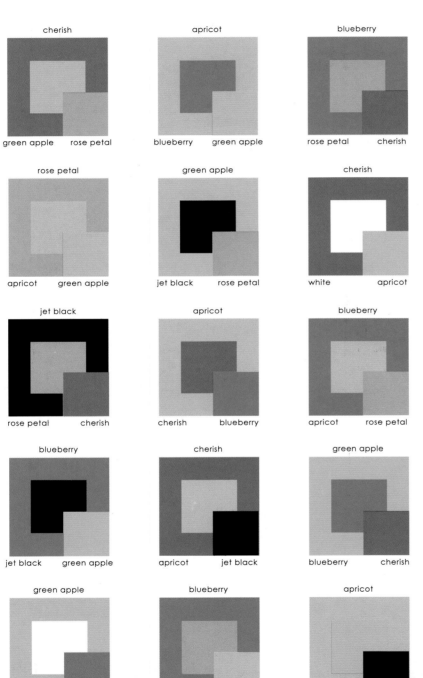

cherish	**apricot**	**blueberry**
green apple · rose petal	blueberry · green apple	rose petal · cherish
rose petal	**green apple**	**cherish**
apricot · green apple	jet black · rose petal	white · apricot
jet black	**apricot**	**blueberry**
rose petal · cherish	cherish · blueberry	apricot · rose petal
blueberry	**cherish**	**green apple**
jet black · green apple	apricot · jet black	blueberry · cherish
green apple	**blueberry**	**apricot**
white · blueberry	rose petal · apricot	green apple · jet black

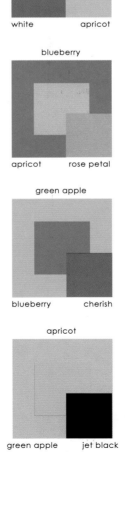

Create It!

College Dorm

Girls Night Out

Best Friends

Sisters

Toddlers

Concerts

Love

Teens

First Apartment

Game Night

Mother and Son

Our Little Sweetie

Dominant Color rose petal

Secondary Color apricot

Accent Colors green apple
and jet black

materials Cardstock (WorldWin)
Patterned Paper, Frame (Chatterbox)
Brads (Making Memories) • Ink • Photo
Corners • Hemp • Silk Flower

Game Night

Dominant Color green apple

Secondary Color cherish

Accent Color blueberry

materials Cardstock (WorldWin) • Stamps,
Ink (Stampin' Up!) • Letters (K&Company)
Frame (Chatterbox) • Ink (Tsukineko)
Ribbon

The best kind of friend is the one
you could sit on a porch with,
never saying a word, and walk
away feeling like that was the best
conversation you have ever had.

Creative Kick-Starts!

Color

Find a Tag Sale in your area and search for old signs, packages, and displays. Keep your eyes open for different combinations of colors.

Journaling

Write a story about your life including the little, everyday things that make you unique.

Design

Imagine the life of a coin, the people it's seen and the places it's gone. Use a coin to mark dates on your pages. For example, use a 2005 penny to remember a graduation or birthday.

Pretty and Pink

a thing of *beauty*
is a *joy forever*

romantic
fun
delicate
soft
sugary
delicious
bright
sentimental
cute
delectable
scrumptious
sweet

flamingo
cupid's blush
pink lemonade
cotton candy
raspberry charm

Sweet Treat

Dominant Color flamingo
Secondary Color cupid's blush
Accent Color cotton candy

materials Patterned Paper (Scrapworks, Junkitz) • Paper Clip (Creative Impressions) Glitter • Ink • Ribbon

A rose speaks of love quietly, in a language known only to the heart.

Color It! Color Combinations

flamingo

cupid's blush   pink lemonade

cotton candy

raspberry charm   cupid's blush

pink lemonade

cupid's blush   cotton candy

cupid's blush

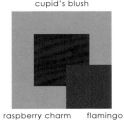

raspberry charm   flamingo

raspberry charm

pink lemonade   cupid's blush

cotton candy

jet black   cupid's blush

pink lemonade

cotton candy   cupid's blush

jet black

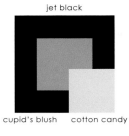

cupid's blush   cotton candy

flamingo

pink lemonade   raspberry charm

cotton candy

flamingo   jet black

pink lemonade

cupid's blush   flamingo

cupid's blush

white   cotton candy

raspberry charm

white   cupid's blush

flamingo

cotton candy   pink lemonade

jet black

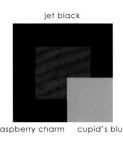

raspberry charm   cupid's blush

Create It!

Valentine's Day

Junior/Senior Prom

First Date

Sweet Tooth

Princess

Dance

Love

Wedding

Engagement

Daughter

Baby Girl

Sisters

*My love for you is a journey;
starting at forever, and
ending at never.*

Creative Kick-Starts!

Color

Become a Kid in a Candy Store! Visit a specialty candy store filled with a rainbow of colorful candy.

Journaling

Write a poem about someone you love. Try writing it in the shape of a heart.

Design

Look through wedding magazines for fun, new trends. Use pearls and silk flowers to create the feel of a wedding or special occasion.

Welcome, Little One

Dominant Color cupid's blush
Secondary Color pink lemonade
Accent Color white

materials Cardstock, Specialty Paper, Stamps, Ink, Eyelets, Glitter (Stampin' Up!) Ribbon

Autumn

Dominant Color flamingo
Secondary Color cupid's blush
Accent Color cotton candy

materials Cardstock (WorldWin) Patterned Paper (Carolee's Creations, Junkitz) • Ink (Tsukineko) • Stamps, Brads (Stampin' Up!) • Glitter • Thread

Timeless and Classic

let your life *lightly dance*
on the edges of *time*
like *dew* on the tip of a *leaf*

—Tagore

elegant
mature
heritage
rich
family
warmth
neutral
refined
regal
classic
sophisticated
smooth

plum passion

midnight

wisteria

dew drop

decadence

Naomi Todhunter Booth
My Grandmother

Some people come into our lives, make footprints on our hearts, and we are never the same.

Life

My Grandmother

Dominant Color jet black
Secondary Colors plum passion and dew drop
Accent Color white

materials Cardstock, Patterned Paper (Chatterbox) · Metal Accent (Die Cuts With A View) · Vellum · Buttons · Ribbon

When someone you love becomes a memory...
the memory becomes a treasure.

plum passion

dew drop   decadence

dew drop

wisteria   midnight

midnight

decadence   dew drop

jet black
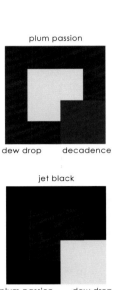
plum passion   dew drop

decadence
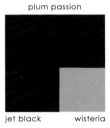
white   dew drop

wisteria

midnight   decadence

midnight

dew drop   plum passion

plum passion

jet black   wisteria

jet black
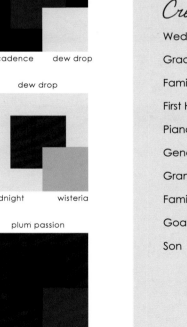
decadence   dew drop

wisteria
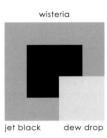
jet black   dew drop

decadence
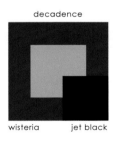
wisteria   jet black

dew drop

midnight   wisteria

jet black

dew drop   plum passion

midnight

plum passion   wisteria

plum passion

jet black   decadence

Create It!

Wedding Anniversary

Graduation

Family Portrait

First Home

Piano Recital

Genealogy

Grandfather

Family

Goals

Son

You can take no credit for beauty at sixteen. But if you are beautiful at sixty, it will be your soul's own doing.

—Marie Stopes

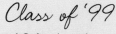

Movie Night

Dominant Color jet black
Secondary Color wisteria
Accent Color dew drop

materials Cardstock (Chatterbox)
Patterned Paper (Junkitz) · Eyelets
(Making Memories) · Raffia

Class of '99

Dominant Color decadence
Secondary Color dew drop
Accent Color plum passion

materials Cardstock (Chatterbox)
Patterned Paper (Junkitz) · Metal
Accents (Making Memories)
Ink · Thread · Class Sticker

Creative Kick-Starts!

Visit the Historic District in your hometown. Be sure to look up as you take a stroll down memory lane. Architecture is a great resource for color and design.

I remember when... Write about something you remember as if it happened yesterday.

Create a family newspaper remembering a recent get-together. Write feature stories and columns. Include a weather report of the day the event took place.

Sultry

to see the *Summer Sky*
is *poetry* —Emily Dickinson

inviting
sticky
sizzling
warm
spirited
blazing
fiery
intense
hot
sweltering
juicy

sunny

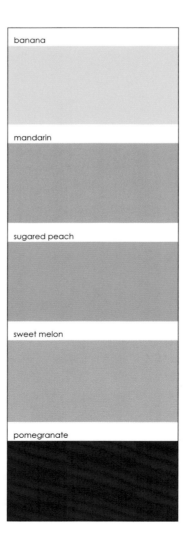

banana

mandarin

sugared peach

sweet melon

pomegranate

Fun in the Sun!

Dominant Color banana
Secondary Colors sugared peach and mandarin
Accent Color white

materials Cardstock (WorldWin)
Patterned Paper (Die Cuts With A View)
Tag (Chatterbox) • Brads (Making Memories) • Ink • Ribbon

Keep your face toward the sunshine and the shadows will fall behind you.

banana

mandarin   pomegranate

sugared peach

banana   mandarin

mandarin

jet black   pomegranate

sweet melon

banana   jet black

jet black

pomegranate   banana

pomegranate

banana   sugared peach

banana

sugared peach   mandarin

pomegranate

white   mandarin

sweet melon

pomegranate   jet black

mandarin

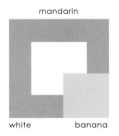

white   banana

banana

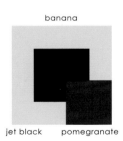

jet black   pomegranate

pomegranate

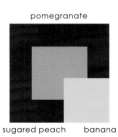

sugared peach   banana

jet black

mandarin   pomegranate

sweet melon

pomegranate   banana

mandarin

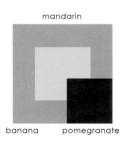

banana   pomegranate

Create It!

Summer at the Beach

Fiesta

Cruise

Fall

Salsa

Island

Travel

Adventure

Bon Voyage

Autumn

Spicy Foods

Pumpkin Carving

Salsa Recipe

Dominant Color mandarin
Secondary Color banana
Accent Color pomegranate

materials Cardstock (WorldWin) • Brads
(Chatterbox) • Ink • Hemp • Ribbon

*If you want a place
in the sun,
you have got to put up
with a few blisters!*

—Abigail Van Buren

Creative Kick-Starts!

Color

Pick up a few back issues of National Geographic magazine. Journey through the pages to far-off lands in search of exotic and brightly colored landscapes. You may even learn a thing or two along the way!

Journaling

Cooking Disasters! Write about a time when your recipe didn't turn out the way you expected.

Design

Take the night off and go out to eat at a Southwestern Restaurant. Look at menus, posters, signs, etc.

Sunbaked and Subtle

thinking of you is like the *Spring*
you bring *love* and *joy*
to *everything*

buttery
warm
comforting
smooth
snug
warming
delicate
inviting
luminous
soft
enlightening
cheerful

sunshine

sweet pea

violet melody

key lime

seashell

Shelzy

Dominant Color sweet pea
Secondary Color violet melody
Accent Colors seashell and
sunshine

materials Cardstock (WorldWin)
Patterned Paper (Frances Meyer, Creative
Imaginations) · Eyelets, Metal Accents
(Making Memories) · Ribbon

*A wee bit of Heaven
drifted down from above,
a handful of happiness,
a heart full of love.*
—Rice

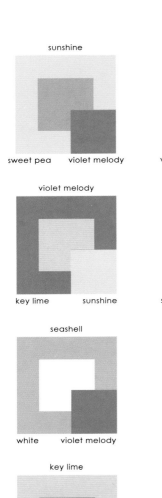
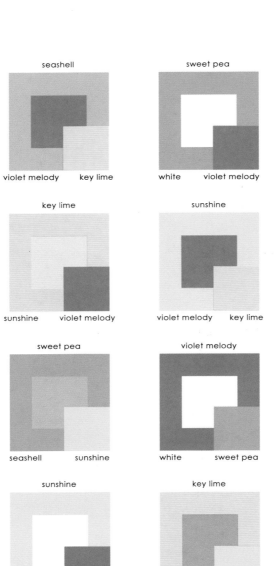
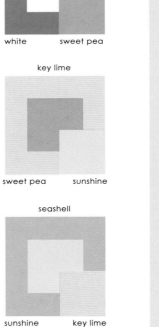
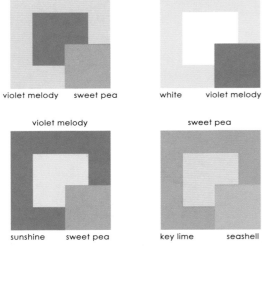

sunshine
sweet pea   violet melody

seashell
violet melody   key lime

sweet pea
white   violet melody

violet melody
key lime   sunshine

key lime
sunshine   violet melody

sunshine
violet melody   key lime

seashell
white   violet melody

sweet pea
seashell   sunshine

violet melody
white   sweet pea

key lime
violet melody   sweet pea

sunshine
white   violet melody

key lime
sweet pea   sunshine

violet melody
sunshine   sweet pea

sweet pea
key lime   seashell

seashell
sunshine   key lime

Create It!

Baby's First Birthday

Day at the Beach

Spring

Nursery Class

Wife

Seaside Vacation

Mother's Day

Easter

Wishes

Sisters

Baby Girl

Sisters are two different flowers from the same garden.

Creative Kick-Starts!

Color

Light a few candles and watch how the colors change when the flame flickers.

Journaling

Signs of Spring... What is it that tells you spring is on its way? Make a list of the sounds and smells that tell you the season's soon to change. What do you love about spring?

Design

Go for a walk and collect small flowers. Press them to create a natural, delicate look for your designs.

"M"

Dominant Color key lime
Secondary Color sunshine
Accent Colors seashell and violet melody

materials Patterned Paper (NRN Designs) Letter Sticker (Creative Imaginations) Flower Accents (Prima Marketing) Cardstock • Ribbon • Brad

Sisters

Dominant Color seashell
Secondary Color sunshine
Accent Colors sweet pea and white

materials Cardstock (WorldWin) Patterned Paper (Creative Imaginations, Frances Meyer) Ink • Brads • Hemp • Thread

A True Friend is the greatest of all blessings.

December 1984 Jordan Valley, Oregon

Warm and Natural

may the *wind*
be always at your *back*

toasted
comfy
creamy
golden
sunny
mellow
inviting
sunbaked
warm
cozy
comfortable
mild

cashmere
green apple
wisteria
pecan
decadence

Smokey

Dominant Color wisteria
Secondary Color green apple
Accent Color pecan

materials Cardstock, Patterned Paper, Tags, Alphabet Stickers (Chatterbox) Eyelets, Metal Tag (Making Memories) Metal Accent (Die Cuts With A View) Vellum · Hemp · Chalk

Autumn is a second spring, where every leaf's a flower.

—Albert Camus

Color It! Color Combinations

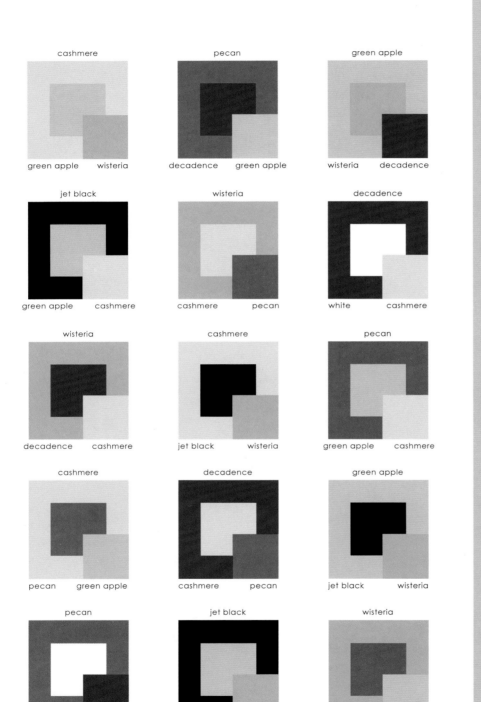

cashmere	pecan	green apple
green apple · wisteria	decadence · green apple	wisteria · decadence

jet black	wisteria	decadence
green apple · cashmere	cashmere · pecan	white · cashmere

wisteria	cashmere	pecan
decadence · cashmere	jet black · wisteria	green apple · cashmere

cashmere	decadence	green apple
pecan · green apple	cashmere · pecan	jet black · wisteria

pecan	jet black	wisteria
white · decadence	green apple · wisteria	pecan · green apple

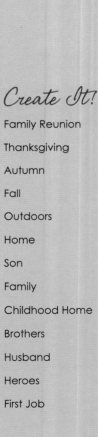

Create It!

Family Reunion

Thanksgiving

Autumn

Fall

Outdoors

Home

Son

Family

Childhood Home

Brothers

Husband

Heroes

First Job

Come said the wind to the leaves one day, come o're the meadows and we will play. Put on your dresses scarlet and gold, for summer is gone and the days grow cold.
—A Children's Song of the 1880's

Creative Kick-Starts!

Color
Take a walk and explore your surroundings. Nature is a great source of color and inspiration.

Journaling
Was there a family gathering you remember vividly? Was it a time when you shared stories and laughter? Write about it.

Design
Nature is very informal and spontaneous, things are usually arranged in odd numbers. In your next project try placing elements in three's or five's.

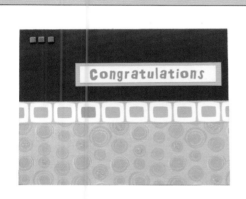

Congratulations

Dominant Color decadence
Secondary Color wisteria
Accent Colors green apple and white

materials Cardstock, Patterned Paper, Sticker (Die Cuts With A View) Brads (Making Memories) · Glitter

Families are Forever

Dominant Color pecan
Secondary Color green apple
Accent Color cashmere

materials Patterned Paper (MM's Designs) · Eyelets (Making Memories) Paper Clip (Creative Impressions) Vellum (Chatterbox) · Brads Ink · Hemp · Thread

Rustic and Earthy

carving out *memories*
one *pumpkin* at a *time*
—Linda LaTourelle

savory
robust
harvest
rich
vintage
autumn
woodsy
comfortable
sturdy
country
reminiscent
wholesome

autumn

maple sugar

pumpkin patch

posh!

russet apple

Within the photo handwriting:
We talked Dad into dressing up as a Pirate for Halloween. As you can see, he really got into the character!
— October 1987

Happy · Halloween

Happy Halloween

Dominant Color maple sugar
Secondary Color russet apple
Accent Colors pumpkin patch and posh!

materials Patterned Paper (Chatterbox, Two Busy Moms) · Eyelets, Metal Tag (Making Memories) · Hemp · Ink Halloween Stamps

Pumpkins in the cornfields, gold among the brown, leaves of rust and scarlet trembling slowly down. Birds that travel southward. Lovely time to play, nothing is as pleasant as an autumn day!

autumn

maple sugar   pumpkin patch

russet apple

posh*!*   maple sugar

posh*!*

maple sugar   russet apple

maple sugar

russet apple   autumn

pumpkin patch

autumn   posh*!*

autumn

white   maple sugar

posh*!*

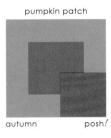

jet black   russet apple

maple sugar

posh*!*   jet black

russet apple

pumpkin patch   autumn

jet black

autumn   pumpkin patch

pumpkin patch

white   posh*!*

autumn

pumpkin patch   russet apple

maple sugar

pumpkin patch   autumn

russet apple

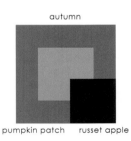

maple sugar   jet black

posh*!*

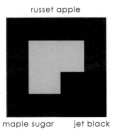

russet apple   pumpkin patch

Create It!

Thanksgiving

Halloween

Pumpkin Carving

Autumn

Outdoors

Fall

Raking Leaves

Family Heritage

Mountain Cabin

Harvest

Camping

You give but little when you give of your possessions. It is when you give of yourself that you truly give.

—Gibran

Thanks!

Dominant Color posh!
Secondary Color russet apple
Accent Color white

materials Cardstock (WorldWin)
Patterned Paper (Chatterbox)
Stamps, Ink, Crystal Effects (Stampin'
Up!) • Hemp • Ribbon • Bottle

On the Farm

Dominant Color posh!
Secondary Color pumpkin patch
Accent Color russet apple

materials Patterned Paper (Die Cuts With
A View, Two Busy Moms) • Brads

Creative Kick-Starts!

Color

Pack up the picnic basket, gather the family and head out to the park for a fun afternoon together. Fall-time puts on a great show of vibrant colors.

Journaling

What's in a Name? Write about the history behind your family name. Does it have an interesting story to tell?

Design

Collect leaves throughout the Autumn season: green, orange, yellow. When dried, leaves make great additions to scrapbook pages or cards.

Soft and Delicate

with a *butterfly kiss*
and a *ladybug hug*
sleep tight little one
like a *bug in a rug*

beloved
mellow
gentle
soft
loving
fragrant
charming
light
mild
cherished
affectionate
quiet

orchid

lullabye

stardust

fairy breeze

forget-me-not

Our Little Girl

Dominant Color orchid
Secondary Color lullabye
Accent Color stardust

materials Cardstock (WorldWin)
Patterned Paper (Creative
Imaginations) • Brads (Stampin' Up!)
Ribbon • Thread • Paper Clip

Springtime bursting out in blossoms,
Bouquets to pick in days to come,
Newborn lambs and frisky colts at play,
Kittens basking in the sun.
—Lynda Tracy

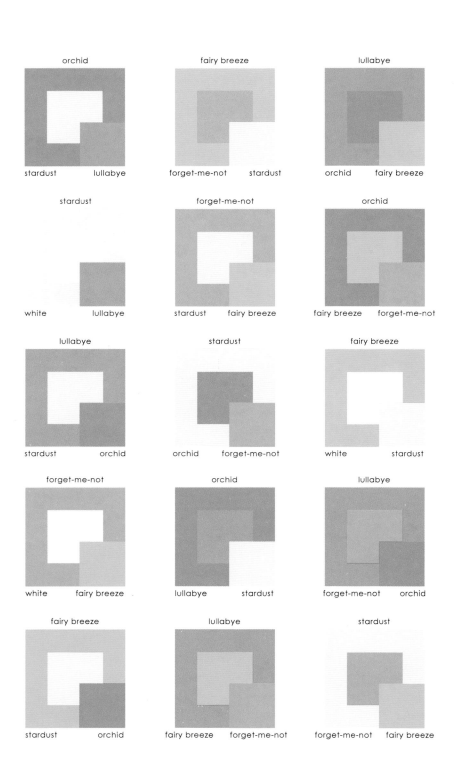

Wynken, Blynken, and Nod one night sailed off in a wooden shoe— sailed on a river of crystal light, into a sea of dew. "Where are you going, and what do you wish?" the old moon asked the three. "We have come to fish for the herring fish that live in this beautiful sea; nets of silver and gold have we," said Wynken, Blynken, and Nod.

—Eugene Field

Creative Kick-Starts!

Color

Indulge in a sweet treat from a specialty ice-cream parlor. Use the colors of ice cream for inspiration.

Journaling

What's baby saying? If your baby could talk what would he or she say? Create quotes for your baby's pictures as if they could talk.

Design

Read a children's story then create your own using your child or yourself as the main character. Let your imagination go and have fun.

Fresh from Heaven

Dominant Color stardust
Secondary Color lullabye
Accent Color jet black

materials Patterned Paper (NRN Designs) • Vellum Quote (Die Cuts With A View) • Cardstock • Ink Ribbon • Brads

Sweet Lil' Girl

Dominant Color stardust
Secondary Color lullabye
Accent Color white

materials Cardstock (WorldWin) Patterned Paper (Frances Meyer, Daisy D's) • Nails (Chatterbox) Ink • Buttons • Thread • Ribbon

Comfy and Cozy

home is where you hang your *heart*

smooth

cozy

warm

country

delicious

creamy

tasty

wholesome

comfortable

homespun

scrumptious

rich

cottage rose

summer lily

emerald lake

wildflower

sunflower

Daddy's girl

Autumn · 2005

Daddy's Girl

Dominant Color cottage rose
Secondary Color summer lily
Accent Color sunflower

materials Patterned Paper (Chatterbox)
Vellum Quote (Die Cuts With A View)
Flower Accents (Prima Marketing)
Brads, Ribbon Slide (Stampin' Up!)
Cardstock · Ink · Ribbon · Chalk

*Family ties are precious threads,
no matter where we roam.
They draw us close to those we love,
and pull our hearts toward home.*

Color It! Color Combinations

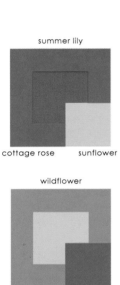

summer lily
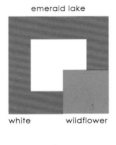
cottage rose   sunflower

emerald lake
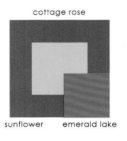
white   wildflower

cottage rose
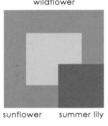
sunflower   emerald lake

wildflower

sunflower   summer lily

sunflower
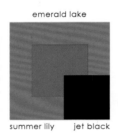
emerald lake   cottage rose

summer lily
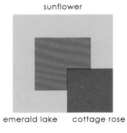
jet black   sunflower

jet black
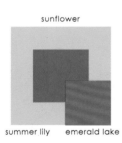
cottage rose   wildflower

emerald lake
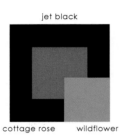
summer lily   jet black

wildflower
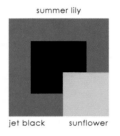
white   cottage rose

sunflower
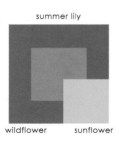
summer lily   emerald lake

cottage rose

emerald lake   sunflower

jet black
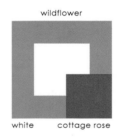
emerald lake   wildflower

summer lily
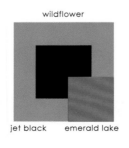
wildflower   sunflower

wildflower
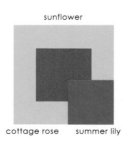
jet black   emerald lake

sunflower
cottage rose   summer lily

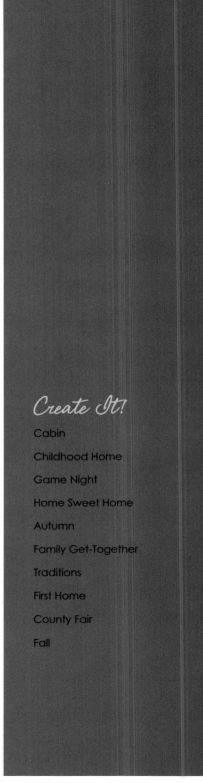

Create It!

Cabin

Childhood Home

Game Night

Home Sweet Home

Autumn

Family Get-Together

Traditions

First Home

County Fair

Fall

Mothers hold their children's hands for a while, their hearts forever.

Creative Kick-Starts!

Color

Take in the sights and sounds of your local county fair. Take a walk on the midway, ride a few rides, and have some cotton candy.

Journaling

Create a *Smile File*. Collect quotes and sayings that make you smile.

Design

Play a game of *Tick-Tack-Toe*, then use the patterns you create for inspiration in your scrapbook pages.

For You

Dominant Color cottage rose
Secondary Color wildflower
Accent Color emerald lake

materials · Patterned Paper (Daisy D's)
Flower Accents (Prima Marketing)
Stamps (Stampin' Up!) · Cardstock
Ink · Ribbon · Glitter

Ain't You Somethin'!

Dominant Color cottage rose
Secondary Color sunflower
Accent Colors emerald lake
and summer lily

materials Cardstock · Ink · Hemp

Tropical

hand in *hand*
through the *sand*

exciting
fresh
exuberant
lively
sprightly
glowing
energy
blooming
peppy
spirited
buoyant
brilliant

aloha	
mango	
pineapple	
flamingo	
sassy lime	

You're Invited!

Dominant Color pineapple
Secondary Color sassy lime
Accent Colors flamingo
and white

materials Cardstock (WorldWin) . Patterned
Paper (BasicGrey) • Marker (Prismacolor)
Fiber (Chatterbox) • Brad (Making Memories)
Stamp (Stampin' Up!) • Hemp • Silk Flower

*Paradise is always
where love dwells.*

—Jean Paul F. Richter

Color It! Color Combinations

aloha

mango   pineapple

flamingo

pineapple   sassy lime

sassy lime

mango   aloha

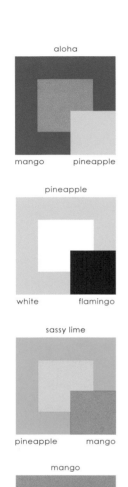

pineapple

white   flamingo

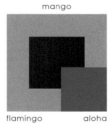

mango

flamingo   aloha

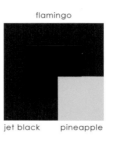

flamingo

jet black   pineapple

sassy lime

pineapple   mango

pineapple

aloha   sassy lime

aloha

sassy lime   pineapple

mango

flamingo   jet black

flamingo

white   sassy lime

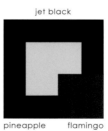

jet black

pineapple   flamingo

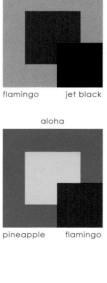

aloha

pineapple   flamingo

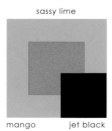

sassy lime

mango   jet black

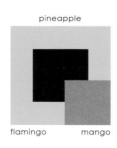

pineapple

flamingo   mango

Party Place Card

Dominant Color pineapple
Secondary Colors aloha
and mango
Accent Colors sassy lime
and flamingo

materials Cardstock (WorldWin) • Eyelet
(Making Memories) • Brad • Ink • Ribbon
Silk Lei

*Look out into the horizon
what is it that you see?
A place where the sun
melts into the trees.
A place where the sky
becomes the sea.*

—Teri Olund

Creative Kick-Starts!

Color

Imagine a lush tropical forest with rich greens and vibrant blossoms against a backdrop of sand and ocean. You can also use tropical fruit as colorful inspiration!

Journaling

You are traveling to a beautiful island, what five things would you take with you? Be creative and don't worry about the necessities, they're already taken care of.

Design

Use items from a local party supply store, such as leis to embellish your projects. Incorporate aquatic shapes in the design. Try using tiny seashells.

Majestic

as we grow old the *beauty* steals *inward*

—Ralph Waldo Emerson

classic
solid
luxurious
polished
mature
distinguished
confident
basic
timeless
sophisticated
professional
expensive

majesty

platinum gray

white pine

chocolate silk

decadence

My Grandparents

Dominant Color decadence
Secondary Color jet black
Accent Colors white pine
and white

materials Cardstock (WorldWin)
Patterned Paper (Die Cuts With A
View, Frances Meyer) • Ink

Irish Wedding Blessing

May God be with you and bless you,
may you see your children's children,
may you be poor in misfortune, and
rich in blessings, and
may you know nothing but
happiness from this day forward.

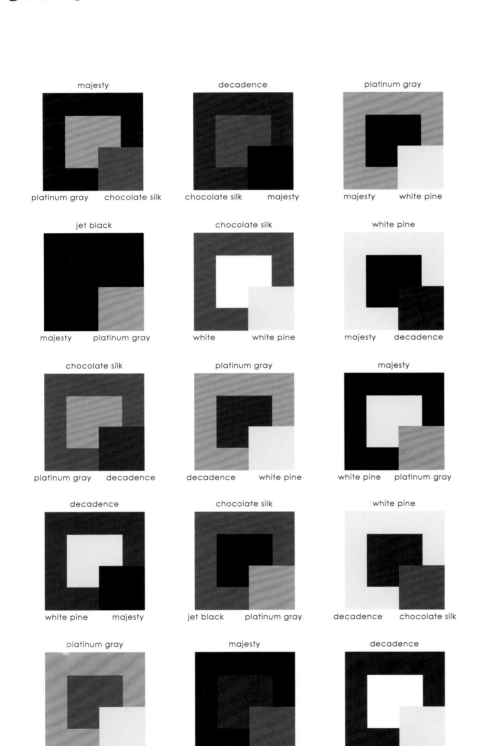

majesty

platinum gray   chocolate silk

decadence

chocolate silk   majesty

platinum gray

majesty   white pine

jet black

majesty   platinum gray

chocolate silk

white   white pine

white pine

majesty   decadence

chocolate silk

platinum gray   decadence

platinum gray

decadence   white pine

majesty

white pine   platinum gray

decadence

white pine   majesty

chocolate silk

jet black   platinum gray

white pine

decadence   chocolate silk

platinum gray

chocolate silk   white pine

majesty

decadence   chocolate silk

decadence

white   white pine

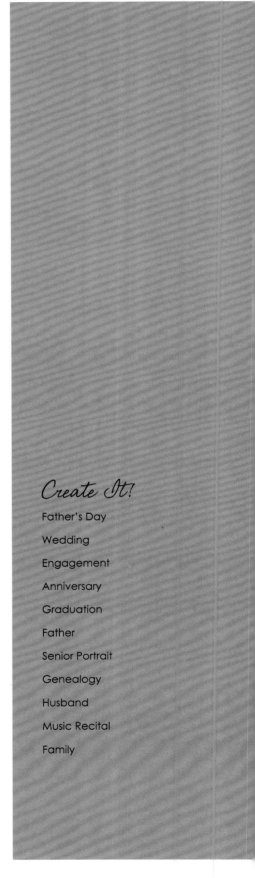

Create It!

Father's Day

Wedding

Engagement

Anniversary

Graduation

Father

Senior Portrait

Genealogy

Husband

Music Recital

Family

Dreams are as real as we believe them to be. Follow your heart wherever it leads you.

—Flavia

Thinking of You

Dominant Color white
Secondary Color white pine
Accent Color majesty

materials Cardstock, Stamps, Ink, Vellum (Stampin' Up!) • Brads

Memories

Dominant Color vanilla bean
Secondary Color majesty
Accent Color white pine

materials Cardstock, Patterned Paper, Vellum, Tags (Chatterbox) • Metal Tag, Eyelets (Making Memories) • Paper Clip (Creative Impressions) • Metal Accent (Die Cuts with a View) • Chalk • Thread

Creative Kick-Starts!

Color

Go for a scenic drive in the mountains and look at the array of beautiful colors nature has to offer.

Journaling

Our Favorite Saying. Does your family have a saying or phrase they use often in certain situations?

Design

Plan to attend a theatrical production in your area. The atmosphere is full of excitement, even at a local high school production. This is a great source of inspiration.

Calming and Tranquil

never be afraid to *sit*
awhile and *think*
—Lorraine Hansberry

heavenly
cool
constant
restful
fresh
dependable
peaceful
serene
soothing
quiet
reassuring
uplifting

bahama blue

paradise

lilac whisper

french lavender

serenity

Baby Boy

Dominant Color serenity
Secondary Color paradise
Accent Color bahama blue

materials Cardstock (WorldWin)
Patterned Paper (Die Cuts With A
View, Creative Imaginations) • Brads
Ink • Hemp • Thread • Photo Corners

*May your day bubble
over with fun!*

Color It! Color Combinations

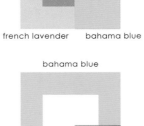

paradise

bahama blue   serenity

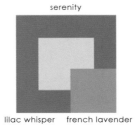

lilac whisper

french lavender   bahama blue

serenity

lilac whisper   french lavender

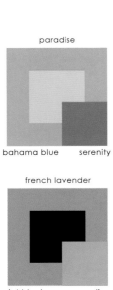

french lavender

jet black   paradise

bahama blue

white   serenity

paradise

serenity   jet black

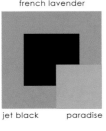

lilac whisper

serenity   french lavender

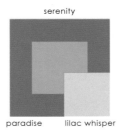

serenity

paradise   lilac whisper

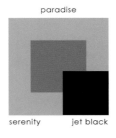

french lavender

lilac whisper   paradise

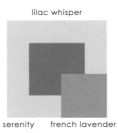

bahama blue

jet black   serenity

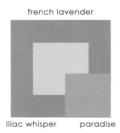

paradise

white   jet black

lilac whisper

french lavender   bahama blue

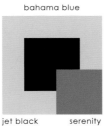

french lavender

lilac whisper   serenity

lilac whisper

paradise   french lavender

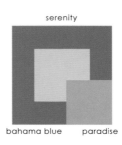

serenity

bahama blue   paradise

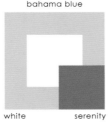

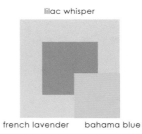

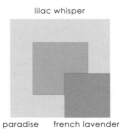

Create It!

Quiet Moments

Sailing

Boating

Seaside Vacation

Rainy Days

Son

Baby Shower

Blue Skies

Bath Time

Brothers

Baby Boy

Ocean

True silence is the rest of the mind, and is to the spirit what sleep is to the body— nourishment and refreshment.

—William Penn

Creative Kick-Starts!

Color

Pack a light lunch, take a walk to the neighborhood park and spend the afternoon watching the birds fly overhead.

Journaling

Write about your ideal day. How does relaxing in a hammock in the back yard without disruptions or phone calls sound?

Design

Take a calming bubble bath. Incorporate bubbles as a design element in your creations.

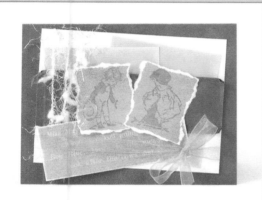

Storybook Note

Dominant Color french lavender
Secondary Color bahama blue
Accent Color white

materials Patterned Paper (Autumn Leaves) • Fiber (Sullivans) • Cardstock Ink • Ribbon

Friend

Dominant Color bahama blue
Secondary Color french lavender
Accent Color paradise

materials Patterned Paper (Chatterbox) Stamps, Embossing Powder, Eyelet, Glitter (Stampin' Up!) • Ink (Tsukineko, Stampin' Up!) Metal Accents (Making Memories) • Cardstock

Whimsical

if you can't *believe*
just *make—believe!*

childlike
subtle
inviting
sweet
fruity
personality
young
engaging
appealing
cheerful
sentimental
vibrant

flutter-by

sherbet

pixie dust

periwinkle

bluebell

Summer 1983

Sunshine

Dominant Color sherbet
Secondary Color flutter-by
Accent Color periwinkle

materials Cardstock (WorldWin)
Metal Accents (Making Memories)
Hemp · Thread

*Spring's greatest joy
beyond a doubt
is when it brings the children out!*

—Edgar A. Guest

flutter-by

sherbet   pixie dust

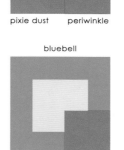

bluebell

flutter-by   sherbet

sherbet

pixie dust   periwinkle

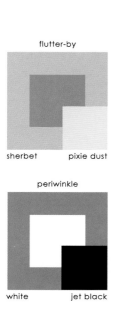

periwinkle

white   jet black

pixie dust

bluebell   flutter-by

bluebell

pixie dust   periwinkle

sherbet

periwinkle   flutter-by

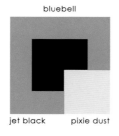

bluebell

jet black   pixie dust

flutter-by

pixie dust   sherbet

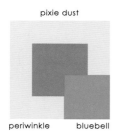

pixie dust

periwinkle   bluebell

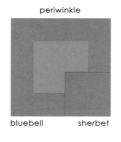

periwinkle

bluebell   sherbet

sherbet

white   pixie dust

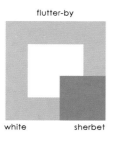

flutter-by

white   sherbet

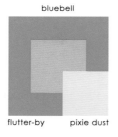

bluebell

flutter-by   pixie dust

pixie dust

periwinkle   flutter-by

Create It!

Mother's Day

Spring

First Day of Spring

Family Fun

Sisters

Youth

Wishes

Spring Break

Slumber Party

Mother and Daughter

Children's Artwork

Friends are like angels,
without any wings.
Blessing our lives,
with the most precious things.

Creative Kick–Starts!

Color

Go fly a kite. Use the shapes and colors for inspiration.

Journaling

Who are the heroines and heroes in your life? Dedicate a scrapbook page to the people who bring joy into your life.

Design

Superstar. Autograph a picture, then list the things that make you unique. Who are your fans, what awards have you achieved?

Friendship

Dominant Color pixie dust
Secondary Color periwinkle
Accent Color sherbet

materials Patterned Paper (Die Cuts With A View, Daisy D's) • Brads Ink • Thread

Angel

Dominant Color sherbet
Secondary Color flutter-by
Accent Color periwinkle

materials Patterned Paper (NRN Designs) Rub-on Letters, Brads (Making Memories) Cardstock • Ribbon • Ink

Polished

light *tomorrow* with *today*
—Elizabeth Barrett Browning

radiant
glossy
sparkling
fun
elegant
sophisticated
gorgeous
delightful
graceful
magnificent
exquisite
youthful

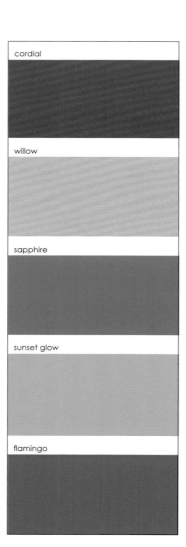

cordial

willow

sapphire

sunset glow

flamingo

Let's Dance!

Dominant Color sapphire
Secondary Colors sunset glow
and willow
Accent Colors cordial and jet black

materials Cardstock (WorldWin) • Stamps, Ink,
Brads (Stampin' Up!) • Flower Brads (Making
Memories) • Ink (Tsukineko) • Photo Corners
Ribbon

How many cares one loses
when one decides not to be
something, but to be someone.

—Coco Chanel

cordial

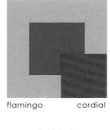

willow   sapphire

sunset glow

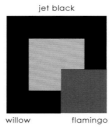

flamingo   cordial

willow

sapphire   sunset glow

sapphire

sunset glow   willow

jet black

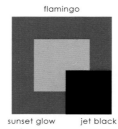

willow   flamingo

flamingo

sunset glow   jet black

willow

white   cordial

cordial

sunset glow   flamingo

sunset glow

flamingo   willow

jet black

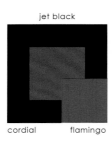

cordial   flamingo

flamingo

willow   sunset glow

sapphire

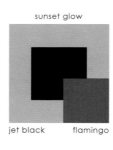

white   cordial

sapphire

flamingo   sunset glow

willow

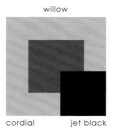

cordial   jet black

sunset glow

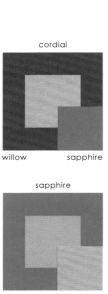

jet black   flamingo

Create It!

Dance

Fashion

Party

Teens

Friends

Daughter

Girls Night Out

First Date

Sisters

Date Night

Father and Daughter

Youth

Wife

A Little Gift

Dominant Color sunset glow
Secondary Colors willow
and white
Accent Color flamingo

materials Cardstock (WorldWin) • Stamps,
Brads (Stampin' Up!) • Ink (Tsukineko,
Stampin' Up!) • Tag (Chatterbox) • Ribbon

*You can dance anywhere,
even if only in your heart.*

Creative Kick-Starts!

Color

Visit a botanical garden and
breathe in the fragrant aroma.
The colors you'll find there will be
wonderfully inspiring.

Journaling

All dressed up... me at my best.
Write about a time when you were
dressed for an evening out on the
town.

Design

Make-up and fragrance displays are
always up-to-date with the latest
trends. Browse through the displays
to see what designs you can create.

Nautical

the best *ships* are *friendships!*

ocean
pleasing
constant
liquid
reliable
rich
dependable
dramatic
deep
cool
refreshing
credible

water polo

yacht green

paradise

regatta

midnight

Daytona
Beach
Florida

安
tranquility

Daytona Beach

Dominant Color jet black
Secondary Color yacht green
Accent Colors paradise and
white

materials Patterned Paper (Die Cuts
With A View) · Stamps, Ink, Brads
(Stampin' Up!) · Cardstock · Ribbon

We cannot direct the
wind but we can
adjust the sails.

Color It! Color Combinations

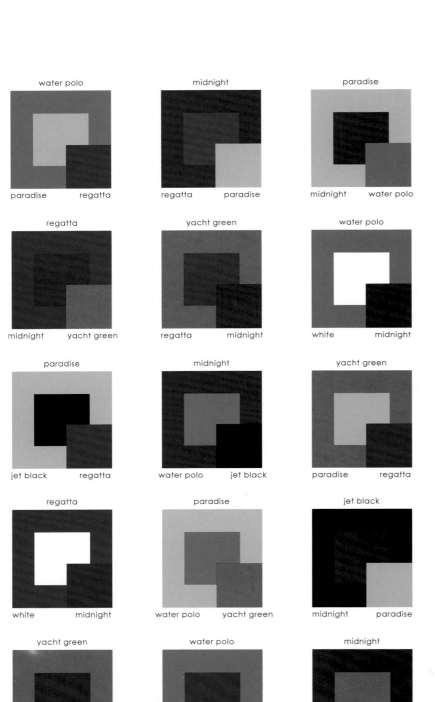

| water polo | midnight | paradise |
| paradise · regatta | regatta · paradise | midnight · water polo |

| regatta | yacht green | water polo |
| midnight · yacht green | regatta · midnight | white · midnight |

| paradise | midnight | yacht green |
| jet black · regatta | water polo · jet black | paradise · regatta |

| regatta | paradise | jet black |
| white · midnight | water polo · yacht green | midnight · paradise |

| yacht green | water polo | midnight |
| midnight · jet black | regatta · paradise | yacht green · water polo |

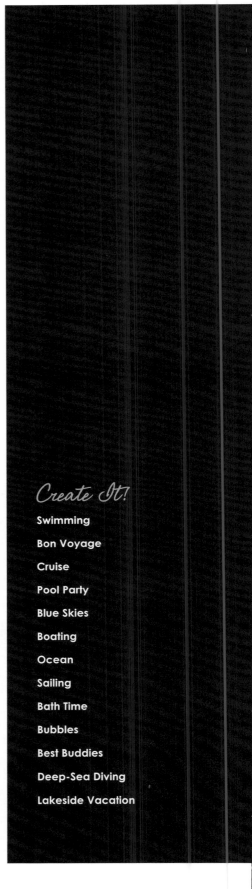

Create It!

Swimming

Bon Voyage

Cruise

Pool Party

Blue Skies

Boating

Ocean

Sailing

Bath Time

Bubbles

Best Buddies

Deep-Sea Diving

Lakeside Vacation

Where the ocean meets the sky, I'll be sailing!

Pool Party!

Dominant Color paradise
Secondary Color regatta
Accent Color white

materials Patterned Paper (Die Cuts With A View) · Ink · Hemp · Ribbon cardstock

Lakeside Vacation

Dominant Color yacht green
Secondary Color midnight
Accent Color paradise

materials Ink (Tsukineko) · Eyelets (Making Memories) · Hemp Textured Cardstock

Creative Kick-Starts!

Color

If you live near an ocean this kick-start's for you. Visit a lighthouse, the views you'll see there will be absolutely breathtaking.

Journaling

Favorite Places. Map out your dream cruise. Where would you like to go, what places would you like to see? Don't worry about budget or transportation, this is your dream, the sky's the limit.

Design

Go to a marina and look at the many different styles of boats. Incorporate the shapes and patterns you find into your next design.

Magical

freckles are
fairies' *kisses*

elegant
enchanting
regal
mystical
nostalgic
fantasy
meditative
spiritual
surreal
creative
inspirational
sophisticated

midnight
purple pansy
amethyst
orchid
berry kissed

Wedding Flowers

Dominant Color midnight
Secondary Colors amethyst and
berry kissed
Accent Colors white and jet black

materials Cardstock (WorldWin) · Patterned
Paper (NRN Designs) · Ink · Brads · Ribbon

*I love her and that's the
beginning of everything.*

—F. Scott Fitzgerald

Color It! Color Combinations

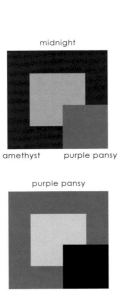

midnight

amethyst   purple pansy

amethyst

white   midnight

berry kissed
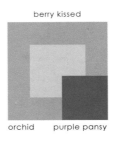
orchid   purple pansy

purple pansy

orchid   jet black

jet black

purple pansy   orchid

orchid
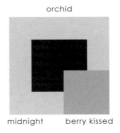
midnight   berry kissed

berry kissed
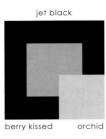
white   purple pansy

midnight

berry kissed   amethyst

amethyst
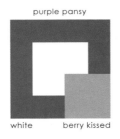
midnight   orchid

jet black
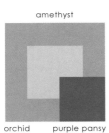
berry kissed   orchid

orchid

jet black   midnight

purple pansy
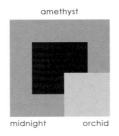
white   berry kissed

amethyst

orchid   purple pansy

midnight

purple pansy   berry kissed

berry kissed

midnight   orchid

Create It!

Wedding

Engagement

Junior/Senior Prom

Wishes

Dreams

Daughter

Little Princess

Dance

Fairy Tale

Sisters

Collections

Mother and Daughter

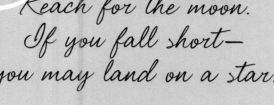

Reach for the moon.
If you fall short—
you may land on a star.

Creative Kick-Starts!

Color

Look for color ideas in children's fantasy books at your local library or bookstore.

Journaling

Storytelling. Write about your photos as if you're writing a fairy tale. Include "Once upon a time..." and "they lived happily ever after."

Design

Go star-gazing and look for designs in the constellations which you can incorporate into your projects. How about using glitter to represent twinkling stars!

Hope

Dominant Color berry kissed
Secondary Color orchid
Accent Color white

materials Rub-ons (Making Memories)
Textured Cardstock · Patterned Vellum
Ribbon · Eyelets · Ink

I Love You

Dominant Color amethyst
Secondary Color midnight
Accent Color white

materials Stamps (Stampin' Up!) · Ink
(Tsukineko) · Metal Accent (Die Cuts With
A View) · Cardstock · Embossing Powder
Rhinestones · Ribbon · Silver Cord · Ink

Light and Airy

angels fly because they take themselves *lightly*

—G.K. Chesterton

wispy

clean

glistening

pure

silent

fragile

delicate

quiet

innocent

peaceful

romantic

soft

spring

cherry blossom

cream puff

sugar plum

moonlight

Michelle & Aaron
August 2002

Engagement

Dominant Color cherry blossom
Secondary Color white
Accent Color sugar plum

materials Patterned Paper (Paper
Adventures) • Paper Clip (Creative
Impressions) • Brads • Chalk • Ribbon
Photo Corners

*Love is like a butterfly,
it goes where it pleases and
it pleases wherever it goes.*

Color It! Color Combinations

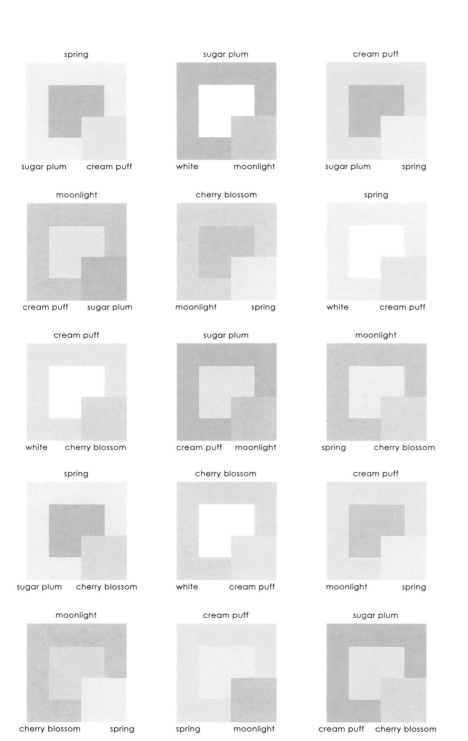

spring
sugar plum · cream puff

sugar plum
white · moonlight

cream puff
sugar plum · spring

moonlight
cream puff · sugar plum

cherry blossom
moonlight · spring

spring
white · cream puff

cream puff
white · cherry blossom

sugar plum
cream puff · moonlight

moonlight
spring · cherry blossom

spring
sugar plum · cherry blossom

cherry blossom
white · cream puff

cream puff
moonlight · spring

moonlight
cherry blossom · spring

cream puff
spring · moonlight

sugar plum
cream puff · cherry blossom

Create It!

Wedding

Baby's Blessing

Baptism

Kite Day

Baby Shower

Easter

Bridal Shower

Tooth Fairy

Daughter

Baby Girl

Baby Boy

*The rustle of the wind
reminds us a Fairy
is near.*

Creative Kick-Starts!

Color

Look up. Find a comfy spot on the grass, lay back and let your imagination go. What shapes are the clouds making? What colors do you see?

Journaling

What if you had all the time in the world, what would you do with it? Would you spend more time with your family?

Design

Create pictures from torn paper. Try a heart to start, then be creative, what other shapes can you make?

Love

Dominant Color moonlight
Secondary Color sugar plum
Accent Color cherry blossom

materials Cardstock (WorldWin) Patterned Paper (Die Cuts With A View) Stamp, Ink (Stampin' Up!) • Frame (Chatterbox) • Brad

Wedding Card

Dominant Color spring
Secondary Color cherry blossom
Accent Color jet black

materials Cardstock (WorldWin) Stamps, Ink (Stampin' Up!) • Ribbon

Youthful

children put a *twinkle* *in your* *eyes* *and a* *smile* *in your* *heart*

young
spirited
playful
fresh
vibrant
innocent
exciting
bright
sunshine
fun
energetic
happy

sweetheart

lemonade

flamingo

caribbean blue

jungle

First Grade

Dominant Color sweetheart
Secondary Color flamingo
Accent Color lemonade

materials Cardstock • Patterned Paper
(Die Cuts With A View) • Stickers (Arctic
Frog) • Ribbon

A rose can say I Love You,
Orchids can enthrall;
But a weed bouquet in a chubby fist,
Oh my, that says it all!

Color It! Color Combinations

sweetheart

lemonade   caribbean blue

flamingo

white   lemonade

sweetheart

caribbean blue   jungle

caribbean blue

jungle   flamingo

jet black

flamingo   lemonade

jungle

lemonade   caribbean blue

lemonade

jet black   caribbean blue

sweetheart

lemonade   flamingo

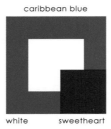

caribbean blue

white   sweetheart

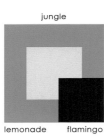

jungle

lemonade   flamingo

flamingo

caribbean blue   lemonade

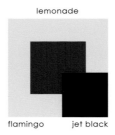

lemonade

flamingo   jet black

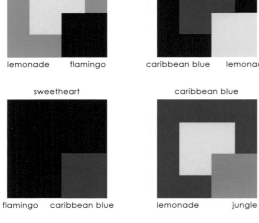

sweetheart

flamingo   caribbean blue

caribbean blue

lemonade   jungle

jet black

sweetheart   lemonade

Create It!

Picnic

Park

Children

School Days

Youth

Friends

Summer Break

Birthday Party

Children's Artwork

Mother and Son

There is a garden in every childhood,
an enchanted place where colors are brighter,
the air softer, and the morning more
fragrant than ever again.

—Elizabeth Lawrence

Happy Birthday!

Dominant Color caribbean blue
Secondary Color sweetheart
Accent Colors lemonade and white

materials Patterned Paper (Die Cuts With A
View) • Sticker (Arctic Frog) • Stamp, Glitter,
Embossing Powder (Stampin' Up!) • Cardstock
Silver Cord

Happy Birthday!

Dominant Color flamingo
Secondary Color lemonade
Accent Color white

materials Cardstock, Patterned Paper
(Arctic Frog) • Stamp, Tag (Stampin'
Up!) • Ink • Ribbon • Silver Cord

Creative Kick-Starts!

Color

Finger painting. Grab the paper
and the paints, now's the time to
become a kid again.

Journaling

Write the titles and descriptions to
your photographs using a brand
new box of crayons.

Design

Play a game you remember from
your childhood like Candyland™
or UNO™. This is a great way to get
your mind thinking creatively.

Rough and Rowdy

I'm in *bug trouble!*

natural
woodsy
dirty
rooted
rustic
forest
masculine
sturdy
outdoors
secure
sheltering
durable

sailor blue

ribbit ribbit

mud puddle

river rock

alpine meadow

Mikey

Dominant Color river rock
Secondary Colors ribbit ribbit
and alpine meadow
Accent Color mud puddle

materials Cardstock (WorldWin) · Patterned
Paper (Die Cuts With A View) · Stamps, Ink,
Brads (Stampin' Up!) · Thread · Hemp

There are four seasons:
Football, Hockey,
Basketball, and Baseball.

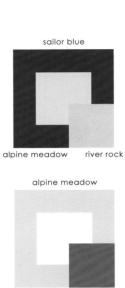

sailor blue

alpine meadow   river rock

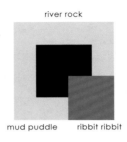

river rock

mud puddle   ribbit ribbit

mud puddle

alpine meadow   river rock

alpine meadow

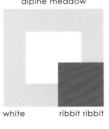

white   ribbit ribbit

ribbit ribbit

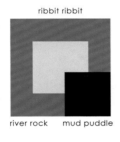

river rock   mud puddle

jet black

river rock   alpine meadow

mud puddle

river rock   alpine meadow

sailor blue

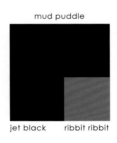

white   ribbit ribbit

mud puddle

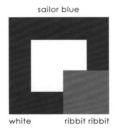

jet black   ribbit ribbit

river rock

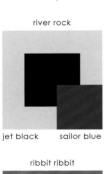

jet black   sailor blue

mud puddle

river rock   jet black

alpine meadow

sailor blue   mud puddle

ribbit ribbit

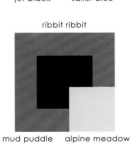

mud puddle   alpine meadow

sailor blue

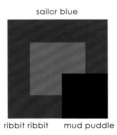

ribbit ribbit   mud puddle

river rock

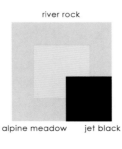

alpine meadow   jet black

Create It!

Son

Buddies

Military

Athletics

Little League

Soccer Practice

The Big Game

Father's Day

Outdoors

Camping

Scouts

Favorite Pet

Backpacking

Baseball

Football

When you're close to the ground
there's more dirt to be found!

The Payette

Dominant Color mud puddle
Secondary Color alpine meadow
Accent Color jet black

materials Cardstock · Tag (Chatterbox)
Hemp · Ink · Thread

Camping Trip

Dominant Color ribbit ribbit
Secondary Color mud puddle
Accent Color jet black

materials Cardstock, Stamps, Ink, Brads
(Stampin' Up!) · Hemp · Thread

Creative Kick-Starts!

Have you ever been to a rodeo?
This is where you can find great
inspiration for your rough and
rowdy designs.

Are we there yet? Write about a
childhood travel experience. Is it a
pleasant memory? Remember the
details: who, what, when, where,
why, how.

Go to a hometown football game
on a Friday night. Be sure to hold on
to your admission tickets, they make
great, inexpensive embellishments.

Sunny and Sweet

laughter brings *Sunshine* into the *home!*

vibrant
lively
energetic
tangy
wild
exciting
sunshine
bright
warm
dramatic
cheerful
hot

strawberry jam

mango

sunflower

sassy lime

cherry pie

Happy Birthday!

Dominant Color mango
Secondary Color sunflower
Accent Colors cherry pie
and sassy lime

materials Cardstock (WorldWin)
Patterned Paper (Colors By Design)
Brad · Ribbon

The sunshine that comes from your heart is warmer than any that comes from the sky.

strawberry jam

sassy lime   sunflower

sassy lime

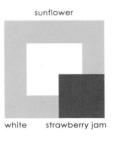

mango   cherry pie

sunflower

white   strawberry jam

jet black

strawberry jam   sassy lime

mango

sunflower   strawberry jam

cherry pie

sassy lime   mango

strawberry jam

mango   sassy lime

sassy lime

strawberry jam   jet black

mango

cherry pie   sassy lime

sunflower

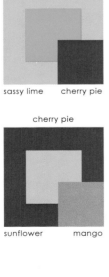

sassy lime   cherry pie

strawberry jam

white   sunflower

jet black

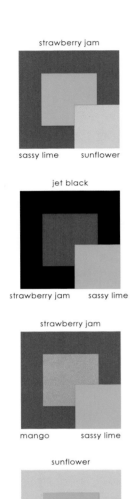

sassy lime   sunflower

cherry pie

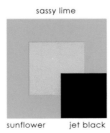

sunflower   mango

sassy lime

sunflower   jet black

sunflower

strawberry jam   sassy lime

Create It!

Summer Vacation

Lazy Days of Summer

Gardening

Movies

Friends

Trip to the Zoo

Birthday Party

School Days

Perfect Lemonade

Dominant Color cherry pie
Secondary Color sunflower
Accent Color jet black

materials Cardstock (WorldWin)
Brad (Making Memories) • Stamps,
Ink, Glitter (Stampin' Up!) • Ink
(Tsukineko) • Ribbon

Good Luck!

Dominant Color sunflower
Secondary Color cherry pie
Accent Color mango

materials Stamps, Ink (Stampin' Up!)
Fibers (Sullivans) • Cardstock
Ribbon • Pencils

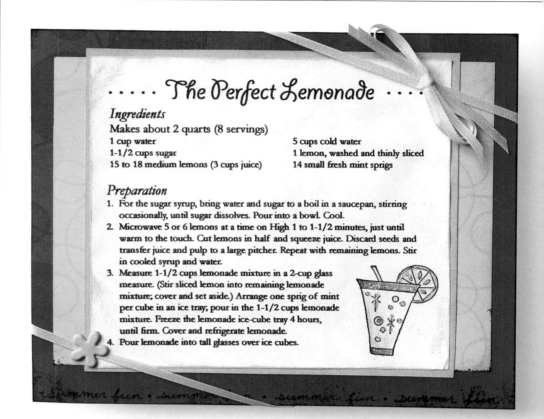

· · · · · The Perfect Lemonade · · · ·

Ingredients

Makes about 2 quarts (8 servings)

1 cup water	5 cups cold water
1-1/2 cups sugar	1 lemon, washed and thinly sliced
15 to 18 medium lemons (3 cups juice)	14 small fresh mint sprigs

Preparation

1. For the sugar syrup, bring water and sugar to a boil in a saucepan, stirring occasionally, until sugar dissolves. Pour into a bowl. Cool.
2. Microwave 5 or 6 lemons at a time on High 1 to 1-1/2 minutes, just until warm to the touch. Cut lemons in half and squeeze juice. Discard seeds and transfer juice and pulp to a large pitcher. Repeat with remaining lemons. Stir in cooled syrup and water.
3. Measure 1-1/2 cups lemonade mixture in a 2-cup glass measure. (Stir sliced lemon into remaining lemonade mixture; cover and set aside.) Arrange one sprig of mint per cube in an ice tray; pour in the 1-1/2 cups lemonade mixture. Freeze the lemonade ice-cube tray 4 hours, until firm. Cover and refrigerate lemonade.
4. Pour lemonade into tall glasses over ice cubes.

*Just a spoonful of sunshine
to brighten your day.*

Creative Kick-Starts!

Color

Visit your local farmers market, you might be surprised at the array of colors you'll find.

Journaling

Take a trip to the zoo, then write out a conversation you might have with your favorite animal.

Design

Create a mosaic of pictures. Start by creating patterns with small photos. Then, if you feel adventurous, cut a larger photo into several smaller pieces to create a miniature work of art.

Refreshing

tubs full of
bubbles
and *bedtime tales*

pristine
ocean
soothing
fresh
serene
tropical
rejuvinating
jewels
peaceful
crisp
cool
quiet

bluegrass

raindrop

lavender sachet

peppermint pizazz

deep ocean

Brothers

Dominant Color lavender sachet
Secondary Color peppermint pizazz
Accent Colors raindrop and white

materials Cardstock (WorldWin) · Patterned Paper (Creative Imaginations, Die Cuts With A View) · Metal Accents (Making Memories) Ribbon

Dear God,
*   Thank you for the baby*
brother, but what I prayed
for was a puppy.

bluegrass

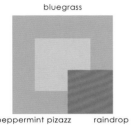

peppermint pizazz　　raindrop

lavender sachet

deep ocean　　peppermint pizazz

raindrop

bluegrass　　deep ocean

peppermint pizazz

white　　bluegrass

bluegrass

raindrop　　peppermint pizazz

deep ocean

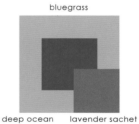

lavender sachet　　jet black

lavender sachet

raindrop　　bluegrass

raindrop

white　　deep ocean

bluegrass

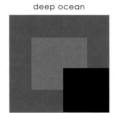

deep ocean　　lavender sachet

deep ocean

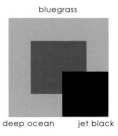

white　　lavender sachet

peppermint pizazz

bluegrass　　jet black

raindrop

lavender sachet　　bluegrass

bluegrass

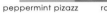

deep ocean　　jet black

raindrop

lavender sachet　　deep ocean

lavender sachet

peppermint pizazz　　raindrop

*Anyone who thinks only sunshine
brings happiness has never
danced in the rain.*

Creative Kick-Starts!

Color Go on a bicycle ride and breathe
the fresh air. It's always a good idea
to take a break from everyday things.

Journaling Describe rain to someone who has
never seen it. Include the five senses:
touch, smell, sound, sight and taste.
Be creative with the last one!

Design Look for good examples of product
packaging designs for chewing gum
or toothpaste at your local grocery
store.

Thanks

Dominant Color deep ocean
Secondary Color lavender sachet
Accent Color peppermint pizazz

materials Patterned Paper, Sticker
(Die Cuts With A View) • Cardstock
(WorldWin) • Stamps, Ink (Stampin' Up!)
Ribbon • Silver Cord • Small Tin

It's a Boy!

Dominant Color bluegrass
Secondary Color raindrop
Accent Colors deep ocean
and white

materials Cardstock (WorldWin)
Patterned Paper (Die Cuts With A
View) • Glitter • Ink • Thread

Fanciful

Swings are angels' wings!

carefree
lovely
splendid
sweet
appealing
joyful
wishful
subtle
dreamy
youthful
imaginative
whimsical

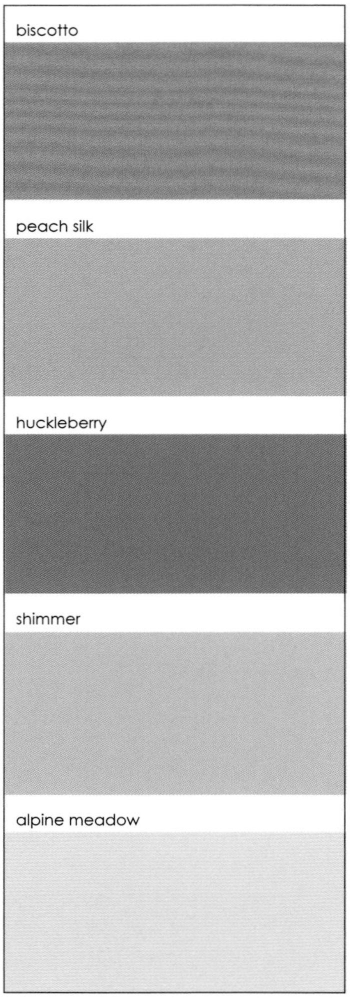

biscotto

peach silk

huckleberry

shimmer

alpine meadow

Our Little Girl

Dominant Color shimmer
Secondary Color peach silk
Accent Color white

materials Cardstock, Vellum (WorldWin)
Patterned Paper (Die Cuts With A View)
Stamps, Ink (Stampin' Up!) · Title
(Chatterbox) · Brads (Chatterbox, Making
Memories) · Photo Corners · Ribbon

Have you ever heard of the sugar-plum tree?
'Tis a marvel of great renown! It blooms on the
shore of the lollipop sea in the garden of shut-
eye town... So come, little child, cuddle closer to
me in your dainty white nightcap and gown, and
I'll rock you away to that sugar-plum tree in
the garden of shut-eye town.
—Eugene Field

huckleberry

peach silk   alpine meadow

shimmer

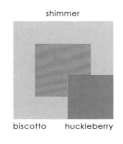

biscotto   huckleberry

alpine meadow

huckleberry   biscotto

peach silk

shimmer   huckleberry

huckleberry

biscotto   shimmer

shimmer

white   peach silk

alpine meadow

biscotto   peach silk

biscotto

white   alpine meadow

peach silk

alpine meadow   shimmer

shimmer

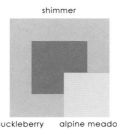

huckleberry   alpine meadow

huckleberry

alpine meadow   peach silk

biscotto

shimmer   huckleberry

huckleberry

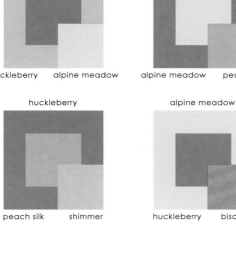

peach silk   shimmer

alpine meadow

huckleberry   biscotto

peach silk

huckleberry   alpine meadow

Create It!

Wishes

Fairy Tale

Children

Spring

Easter

Candy

Dreams

Dance

Daughter

Love

Friends

Little Princess

Grandmother

Mother

Inside Jokes

Dominant Color huckleberry
Secondary Color alpine meadow
Accent Colors peach silk and white

materials Cardstock (WorldWin) • Title, Tag (Chatterbox) • Ink • Eyelets (Making Memories) Ribbon • Hemp • Candy

Leave room in your garden for Fairies to dance.

Creative Kick-Starts!

Color

Lose yourself in a great animated classic fairy tale movie. Let the beautiful artwork be a source of inspiration for your own creations.

Journaling

Wishing well. Throw a penny in a wishing well then make a wish. Write about what you wished for.

Design

Paper Dolls. Use this as a design element in your next project. If you're scrapbooking a birthday party how about making a paper party hat to add to the photograph?

Refined

the purpose of *life*
is a life of *purpose*

stylish
taste
dramatic
enlightened
upscale
cultured
luxurious
rich
educated
quality
fashionable
perfection

chapel hill

country club

palm beach

bay harbor

cypress

Great is the man who holds his child's heart close with utmost love and tenderness.

—Linda LaTourelle

Wisdom

Dominant Color palm beach
Secondary Color country club
Accent Colors chapel hill and bay harbor

materials Cardstock (WorldWin)
Stamps, Ink, Brads (Stampin' Up!)
Frame, Tag (Chatterbox) • Ribbon

Downtown

Dominant Color bay harbor
Secondary Colors country club, chapel hill and palm beach
Accent Color jet black

materials Cardstock (WorldWin) • Stamps,
Brads (Stampin' Up!) • Ink (Tsukineko,
Stampin' Up!) • Photo Corners

Creative Kick-Starts!

Color

Attend the opening of an exhibit at your local art museum and look at the colors that surround you.

Journaling

Write a thank-you letter to someone you love. You can either send it to them or use it in your scrapbook, it's your choice.

Design

Visit an upscale furniture store. Take note of the textures and patterns, can you incorporate any of them into your own creations?

downtown

main street

Boise

PHOTO. *the art of capturing the past.*

Rich and Creamy

friends are
the *chocolate chips*
of *life!*

smooth

cozy

warm

refined

delicious

tasty

scrumptious

wholesome

elegant

comfortable

classic

rich

marionberry
butterscotch
vanilla bean
panache
toffee crunch

Our Home

Dominant Color marionberry
Secondary Color butterscotch
Accent Color panache

materials Cardstock (WorldWin) • Patterned
Paper (Autumn Leaves) • Title, Brads (Chatterbox)
Ink • Photo Corners • Ribbon • Eyelets

*Four walls may make a house
but love makes a home.*

Color It! Color Combinations

marionberry

butterscotch   vanilla bean

panache

vanilla bean   toffee crunch

marionberry

white   butterscotch

butterscotch

panache   marionberry

vanilla bean

marionberry   toffee crunch

toffee crunch

marionberry   vanilla bean

vanilla bean

butterscotch   panache

jet black

butterscotch   marionberry

panache

marionberry   butterscotch

toffee crunch

jet black   butterscotch

marionberry

vanilla bean   jet black

butterscotch

panache   vanilla bean

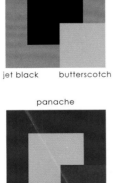

panache

butterscotch   marionberry

vanilla bean

panache   toffee crunch

marionberry

butterscotch   panache

Create It!

Weekend at the Cabin

Steamy Cup of Cocoa

Best Friends

Mother

Grandmother

Autumn

Fall

Home

Winter Days

Family Get-Together

Grandparents sort of sprinkle stardust over the lives of little children.

—Alex Haley

Creative Kick-Starts!

Color

Freshly baked cookies... You'll be surprised at the memories that will come to you when you're surrounded by the aroma of freshly baked cookies.

Journaling

Relax, sit back in your easy chair in front of a warm crackling fire. Think of the things that make you feel warm and cozy.

Design

Visit a coffee shop and look at their signs and promotional materials. While you're there grab a cup of your favorite warm drink.

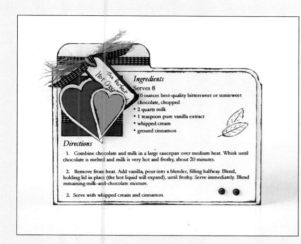

Hot Chocolate Recipe

Dominant Color vanilla bean
Secondary Color panache
Accent Colors marionberry and butterscotch

materials Cardstock (WorldWin)
Stamps, Ink, Brads (Stampin' Up!)
Ribbon · Hemp

Welcome Home

Dominant Color butterscotch
Secondary Color marionberry
Accent Color panache

materials Cardstock (WorldWin)
Stamps, Brads, Ink (Stampin' Up!)
Thread · Ribbon · Key Charm

Bold and Powerful

where your *treasure* is
there will your *heart* be

dynamic
strong
daring
robust
heavy
mature
authority
forceful
energy
substantial
basic
confident

jet black

corporate blue

power red

posh!

midnight

Fireworks

Dominant Colors power red
and jet black
Secondary Color posh!
Accent Color corporate blue

materials Cardstock (WorldWin) · Patterned
Paper (Die Cuts With A View, Keeping Memories
Alive, Chatterbox) · Metal Accents (Making
Memories) · Hemp

Whatever you can do or
dream you can, begin it.
Boldness has genius, power,
and magic in it.

—von Goethe

jet black

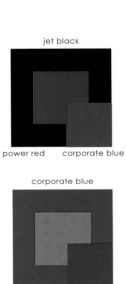

power red   corporate blue

posh!

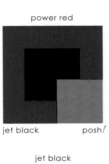

jet black   midnight

power red

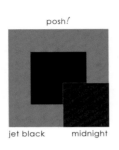

jet black   posh!

corporate blue

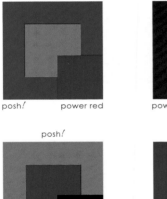

posh!   power red

midnight

power red   jet black

jet black

midnight   power red

posh!

power red   jet black

power red

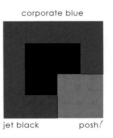

white   corporate blue

corporate blue

jet black   posh!

midnight

white   posh!

jet black

posh!   power red

posh!

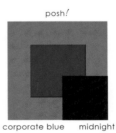

corporate blue   midnight

corporate blue

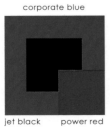

jet black   power red

midnight

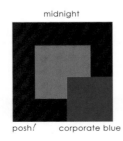

posh!   corporate blue

power red

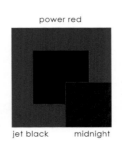

jet black   midnight

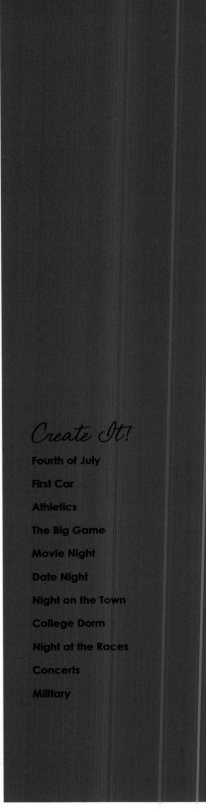

Create It!

Fourth of July

First Car

Athletics

The Big Game

Movie Night

Date Night

Night on the Town

College Dorm

Night at the Races

Concerts

Military

> *Try not to become a man of success, but rather try to become a man of value.*
> —**Albert Einstein**

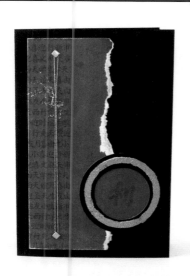

Note Card

Dominant Color jet black
Secondary Color power red
Accent Color metallic gold

materials Patterned Paper (Creative Imaginations) · Frame (Chatterbox) Ink (Tsukineko) · Brads (Making Memories) · Cardstock · Embossing Powder · Gold Cord

Cruisin'

Dominant Color corporate blue
Secondary Color jet black
Accent Colors power red and white

materials Cardstock (WorldWin) Patterned Paper (Creative Imaginations, Karen Foster) · Ink · Brads · Ribbon

Creative Kick-Starts!

Check out a local automotive dealership for their promotional materials and advertisements which display the latest vehicles.

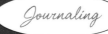

Write about your photographs as if you are a sports broadcaster reporting the big game.

Check out your favorite college or professional sports team colors and logos for design ideas.

Winter Traditions

the *ornaments* of our **home** are the *friends* that gather there

holiday

snow

traditions

home

comfy

packages

family pine

winter

christmas

sentimental

cozy

sweetheart

jolly holly

vanilla bean

l'amour

angel frost

Snow Day!

Dominant Color jolly holly
Secondary Colors angel frost
and jet black
Accent Color vanilla bean

materials Cardstock (WorldWin)
Patterned Paper (Die Cuts With A View)
Paper Clip (Creative Impressions) · Ink
Ribbon

*Even when it's cold outside
our memories keep us warm.*

l'amour

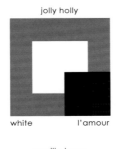

angel frost   vanilla bean

jolly holly

white   l'amour

sweetheart

vanilla bean   jolly holly

sweetheart

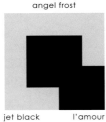

white   jolly holly

vanilla bean

l'amour   jolly holly

angel frost

vanilla bean   l'amour

angel frost

jet black   l'amour

jet black

l'amour   angel frost

l'amour

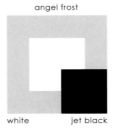

white   vanilla bean

vanilla bean

jolly holly   angel frost

jolly holly

vanilla bean   sweetheart

angel frost

white   jet black

l'amour

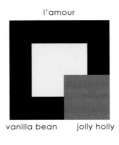

vanilla bean   jolly holly

sweetheart

jolly holly   angel frost

jet black

vanilla bean   sweetheart

Create It!

Christmas

Snow Day

Christmas Traditions

Snow Angels

Skiing

Snowman

Home for the Holidays

Christmas Tree

Take the cookies from the oven,
    warm and spicy made with lovin'.
Hang the holly wreath to say,
    all are welcome on this day.
Place the star atop the tree,
    way up high for all to see.
Fill the season with good cheer,
    Santa Claus will soon be here!

—Lynda Tracy

Merry Christmas

Dominant Color sweetheart
Secondary Color jolly holly
Accent Color vanilla bean

materials Cardstock (WorldWin)
Patterned Paper (Die Cuts With A
View) • Hemp

Christmas Party

Dominant Color sweetheart
Secondary Color white
Accent Color jolly holly

materials Cardstock (WorldWin)
Patterned Paper (Die Cuts With
A View) • Ink • Hemp
Thread • Christmas Stamp

Creative Kick-Starts!

Color

Throw on your coat, some mittens, a good pair of boots and build a snowman. For those of you who live in warmer areas use shaved ice as inspiration!

Journaling

Rewrite *The Twelve Days of Christmas* to fit your family!

Design

Use your gift-wrapping paper for great design ideas in your scrapbook layouts and cards. (Note: gift wrap may not be acid free)

Merry Christmas!

Join us for a
Christmas Celebration...

December 22, 2003
Seven o'clock pm
Michelle's House
806 North 15th Street
Bridgetower Apartments

Bodacious '80s

born in the USA... long ago!

radical
mint
awesome
totally
gnarley
bogus
yo
tubular
stoked
cool
for sure
man

| razzle berry |
| white |
| jet black |
| neon yellow |
| bright lime |

Good Times

Dominant Color jet black
Secondary Color razzle berry
Accent Colors neon yellow
and bright lime

materials Cardstock (WorldWin) · Patterned Paper
(Keeping Memories Alive) · Tag (Chatterbox)
Stamps, Ink, Brads (Stampin' Up!) · Ribbon

*Smile, you may be a blessing
to someone today!*

Color It! Color Combinations

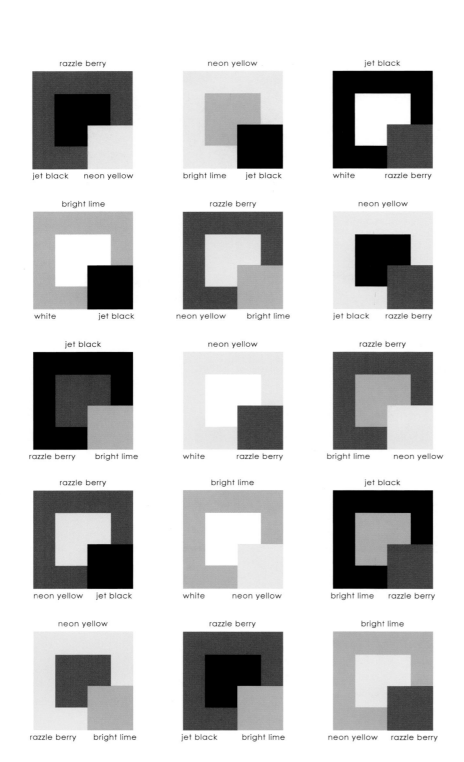

razzle berry	neon yellow	jet black
jet black / neon yellow	bright lime / jet black	white / razzle berry
bright lime	razzle berry	neon yellow
white / jet black	neon yellow / bright lime	jet black / razzle berry
jet black	neon yellow	razzle berry
razzle berry / bright lime	white / razzle berry	bright lime / neon yellow
razzle berry	bright lime	jet black
neon yellow / jet black	white / neon yellow	bright lime / razzle berry
neon yellow	razzle berry	bright lime
razzle berry / bright lime	jet black / bright lime	neon yellow / razzle berry

Create It!

Rock Music

Leg Warmers

Skateboards

Boom Box

Break Dancing

Big Hair and Hairspray

Ski Vests

It's the smile that keeps me outta trouble!

Love

Dominant Color jet black
Secondary Color razzle berry
Accent Color white

materials Cardstock, Stamps, Ink
(Stampin' Up!) · Ribbon

Smiley

Dominant Color bright lime
Secondary Color white
Accent Colors razzle berry
and jet black

materials Cardstock (WorldWin)
Patterned Paper (Keeping Memories
Alive) · Brads (Making Memories)
Ink · Photo corners · Ribbon

Creative Kick-Starts!

Color — Stop by a video rental store and pick up your favorite classic 1980's movie. Pop some popcorn, sit back, relax and enjoy the show.

Journaling — *Backward day.* Write a story but in reverse. Start at the end and work your way to the beginning.

Design — Polka Dots were everywhere in the 1980's. Try incorporating them into your scrapbook pages and cards.

Outta Sight '70s

twinkling with *mischief!*

hunk
happenin'
right on
chill
rockin'
wicked
far out
foxy
jive
skinney
backatcha
you dig?

orange crush

panache

strawberry jam

cypress

sunflower

Peek–a–Boo!

Dominant Color panache
Secondary Color orange crush
Accent Colors cypress and white

materials Cardstock (WorldWin) • Stamps,
Ink (Stampin' Up!) • Hemp • Thread

Precious and priceless, lovable too,
the world's sweetest miracle
is sweet little you.

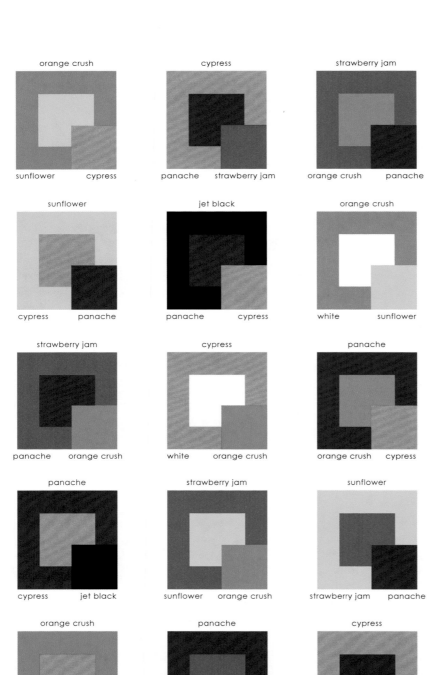

orange crush

sunflower   cypress

cypress

panache   strawberry jam

strawberry jam

orange crush   panache

sunflower

cypress   panache

jet black

panache   cypress

orange crush

white   sunflower

strawberry jam

panache   orange crush

cypress

white   orange crush

panache

orange crush   cypress

panache

cypress   jet black

strawberry jam

sunflower   orange crush

sunflower

strawberry jam   panache

orange crush

cypress   sunflower

panache

strawberry jam   cypress

cypress

panache   sunflower

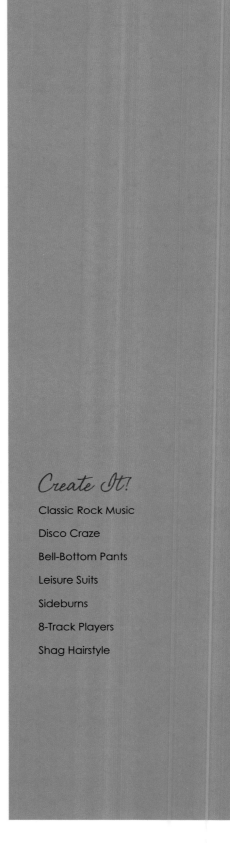

Create It!

Classic Rock Music

Disco Craze

Bell-Bottom Pants

Leisure Suits

Sideburns

8-Track Players

Shag Hairstyle

Live for those who love you.

Honeymoon in California 1976

California

Dominant Color cypress
Secondary Color panache
Accent Color orange crush

materials Cardstock (Chatterbox, WorldWin) • Brads (Making Memories) Ink • Photo Corners • Thread

Our Wedding

Dominant Color jet black
Secondary Color cypress
Accent Color white

materials Cardstock, Patterned Paper, Vellum, Frame (Chatterbox) Brads (Making Memories) • Silver Cord • Ribbon

Creative Kick-Starts!

Color

A great resource for colors in the 1970's is to look at fashion. It might be a little scary at first with all the polyester but you'll get through it alright!

Journaling

What was I thinking? Write about a time when you did, said or wore something silly, then later wondered what you were thinking.

Design

What's a Disco without the mirror ball? Use glitter or sequins to create the affect of mirrors.

Our Wedding 1976

Kevin & Lynda

Groovy '60s

you're only *young once*
but you can be *immature forever!*

funky

primo

jazzed

copasetic

hangin fab

psychadelic

blast

solid

decked out

no way

hep

violet melody
pineapple
flamingo
electric lime
tangerine

Our Best Memories

Dominant Color violet melody
Secondary Colors electric lime
and flamingo
Accent Colors pineapple and tangerine

materials Cardstock (WorldWin) • Patterned
Paper (Keeping Memories Alive, BasicGrey)
Title (Chatterbox) • Fibers (Sullivans) • Ink
Photo Corners • Button • Thread

I'm not old...
I'm a recycled teenager!

Color It! Color Combinations

violet melody

pineapple   flamingo

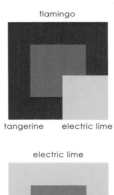

tangerine

electric lime   violet melody

flamingo

tangerine   electric lime

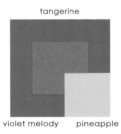

pineapple

flamingo   tangerine

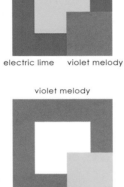

violet melody

white   electric lime

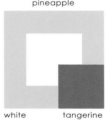

electric lime

violet melody   pineapple

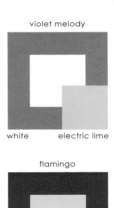

tangerine

violet melody   pineapple

flamingo

pineapple   violet melody

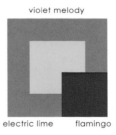

pineapple

white   tangerine

electric lime

white   violet melody

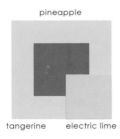

pineapple

tangerine   electric lime

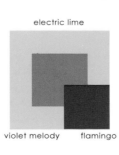

violet melody

electric lime   flamingo

flamingo

electric lime   violet melody

violet melody

pineapple   tangerine

electric lime

violet melody   flamingo

Create It!

Muscle Cars

Hippies

Go-Go Boots

Flower Power

Smiley Face

Vietnam War

Surfing

Days Gone By

Lying on beds of soft, green grass,
Little eyes turned to the sky,
Watching fluffy, cotton clouds
As they slowly pass on by.

—Lynda Tracy

Creative Kick-Starts!

Color

Rock-n-Roll records of the 1960's are known for their outrageous colors, try finding a few and using them as inspiration.

Journaling

Friday the Thirteenth! Write about an unusual or crazy day you had when everything seemed to be out of the ordinary.

Design

Private Investigator. Shoot your photographs as if you're trying not to be seen. Include partial bushes and buildings in the picture frames.

Friends

Dominant Color tangerine
Secondary Color white
Accent Color electric lime

materials Cardstock (WorldWin) • Patterned
Paper (Die Cuts With A View, Chatterbox)
Brads (Stampin' Up!, Chatterbox) • Stamps,
Ink (Stampin' Up!) • Fibers (Sullivans)

First Grade

Dominant Color electric lime
Secondary Color pineapple
Accent Colors flamingo
and tangerine

materials Cardstock (WorldWin) • Patterned
Paper (BasicGrey) • Brads (Making Memories)
Numbers (K&Company) • Buttons • Thread
Ink • Paper Clip • Photo Corners • Ribbon

Be-Bop! '50s

blue jeans...
worn by *time*
faded by *love*

cherry
nifty
cookin'
right on
swell *flip*
unreal
hip
snazzy
keen
daddy-o
neato

goodnight
pink lemonade
key lime
cashmere
jet black

Baby

Dominant Color pink lemonade
Secondary Color key lime
Accent Color goodnight

materials Patterned Paper (me and my BIG
ideas) • Cardstock, Vellum (WorldWin) • Letters
(K&Company) • Fibers (Sullivans) • Ink • Thread
Paper Clip • Buttons • Ribbon

Life's a Bowl of Cherries!

Color It! Color Combinations

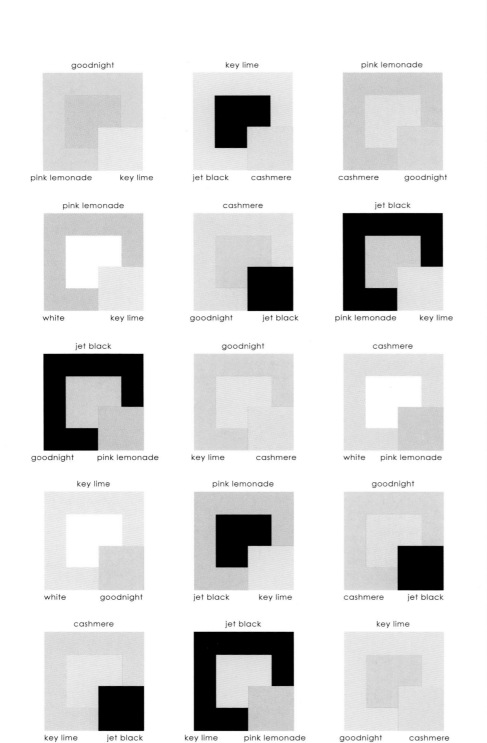

goodnight

pink lemonade | key lime

key lime

jet black | cashmere

pink lemonade

cashmere | goodnight

pink lemonade

white | key lime

cashmere

goodnight | jet black

jet black

pink lemonade | key lime

jet black

goodnight | pink lemonade

goodnight

key lime | cashmere

cashmere

white | pink lemonade

key lime

white | goodnight

pink lemonade

jet black | key lime

goodnight

cashmere | jet black

cashmere

key lime | jet black

jet black

key lime | pink lemonade

key lime

goodnight | cashmere

Create It!

Rock-n-Roll Music

Drive-In Movies

Science Fiction

Saddle Shoes

Poodle Skirts

Korean War

Blue Jeans

With the smell of honeysuckle
I remember days gone by...
I was jumping fences,
My how time does fly.

Creative Kick–Starts!

Color

Have lunch at a retro diner. Be sure to take note of the colors used in menus and promotional signs.

Journaling

Space travel. Write a science fiction story about a day in your life when strange things happened that you couldn't explain.

Design

Rock-n-Roll. Brainstorm several different ways you could incorporate the shape of a music record in your scrapbook layouts.

50th Anniversary

Dominant Color goodnight
Secondary Color jet black
Accent Color cashmere

materials Cardstock (WorldWin)
Frame (Chatterbox) • Numbers
(K&Company) • Stamp, Ink
(Stampin' Up!)

Precious

Dominant Color pink lemonade
Secondary Color jet black
Accent Color key lime

materials Cardstock, Vellum (WorldWin)
Patterned Paper (Daisy D's, BasicGrey)
Brads (Making Memories) • Ink
Photo Corners • Ribbon

Swingin' '40s

memories are like *keepsakes*
always *treasured*

jumpin'
swell
hep cat
swanky
keen
hip
hubba hubba
snazzy
doodlebug
humdinger
jolly up

l'amour

sailor blue

smoky taupe

lipstick red

bittersweet

Sisters

Dominant Color jet black
Secondary Color l'amour
Accent Colors lipstick red
and bittersweet

materials Cardstock (WorldWin, Chatterbox)
Patterned Paper (BasicGrey) • Fibers (Sullivans)
Paper Clip (Creative Impressions) • Ink • Photo
Corners • Ribbon Rose

Count your life by smiles, not tears.
Count your age by friends, not years.

Color It! Color Combinations

l'amour

smoky taupe • sailor blue

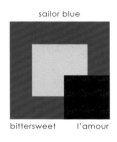

bittersweet

sailor blue • lipstick red

sailor blue

bittersweet • l'amour

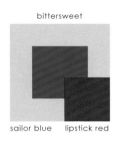

bittersweet

lipstick red • sailor blue

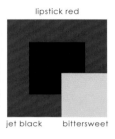

lipstick red

jet black • bittersweet

smoky taupe

l'amour • lipstick red

l'amour

jet black • bittersweet

sailor blue

l'amour • smoky taupe

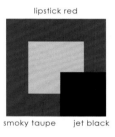

lipstick red

smoky taupe • jet black

smoky taupe

sailor blue • lipstick red

jet black

smoky taupe • l'amour

l'amour

sailor blue • bittersweet

lipstick red

bittersweet • smoky taupe

bittersweet

l'amour • jet black

smoky taupe

jet black • l'amour

Create It!

Swing Dancing

Big Band Era

The Jitterbug

Zoot Suits

Bobby-Soxers

WWII

Electric Train Sets

You know you're getting old when the candles cost more than the cake.
—Bob Hope

I grew up with six brothers. That's how I learned to dance... waiting for the bathroom.
—Bob Hope

Grandpa

Dominant Color lipstick red
Secondary Color bittersweet
Accent Color smoky taupe

materials Cardstock (WorldWin)
Patterned Paper (me and my BIG ideas)
Ribbon • Chalk

Journey

Dominant Color smoky taupe
Secondary Colors l'amour
and jet black
Accent Colors sailor blue
and lipstick red

materials Cardstock (WorldWin)
Patterned Paper (Die Cuts With A View,
BasicGrey) • Brad • Ink • Ribbon

Creative Kick-Starts!

Color

Visit with someone who lived during the 1940's. Ask them to share memories of trends in color such as fashion and home furnishings.

Journaling

Interview a WWII veteran and write their story. Print it on ivory-colored paper and chalk the edges, this will create a great vintage look.

Design

Find design inspiration by visiting a vintage airplane museum.

Jazzy '30s

the *years* teach much
which the *days*
never knew

—Ralph Waldo Emerson

live wire

unreal

hot dawg

jolly up

keen

jitterbug

baby

big idea

jive

lollapalooza

bowl of cherries

truckin'

ruby
paradise
bisque
garland
decadence

Family

Dominant Color ruby
Secondary Color garland
Accent Color bisque

materials Cardstock (WorldWin) • Patterned
Paper (Lasting Impressions, me and my BIG
ideas) • Ink • Brads • Hemp • Ribbon

*Families are like quilts, lives
pieced together, stitched with
memories, and bound by love.*

Color It! Color Combinations

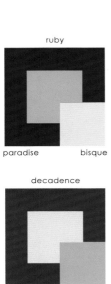

ruby
paradise   bisque

bisque
garland   decadence

garland
ruby   paradise

decadence
bisque   paradise

jet black
decadence   garland

paradise
ruby   jet black

garland
jet black   decadence

bisque
ruby   decadence

ruby
garland   bisque

paradise
decadence   bisque

ruby
bisque   garland

jet black
garland   ruby

ruby
garland   paradise

bisque
decadence   ruby

decadence
paradise   garland

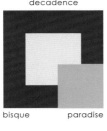
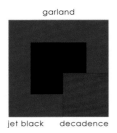
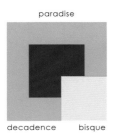
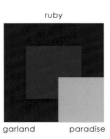
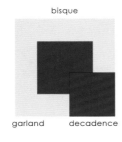

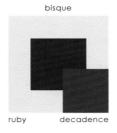

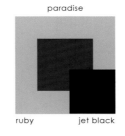

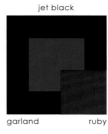
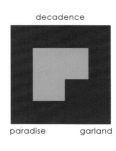

Create It!

Jazz Music

Roller Skating Rinks

Radio Shows

Song and Dance Films

Stickball

The Great Depression

Wing-Tipped Shoes

A child fills a place in your heart you never knew was empty.

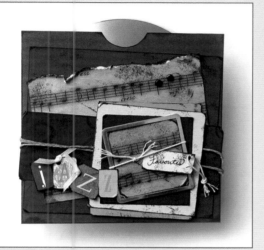

Jazz Favorites
Dominant Color garland
Secondary Colors decadence and ruby
Accent Colors bisque and paradise

materials Cardstock (WorldWin)
Patterned Paper (EK Success, Two Busy Moms) • Brads (Making Memories)
Letters (K&Company) • Ink • Metal Tag • Hemp • Ribbon

Play it Again!
Dominant Color decadence
Secondary Color bisque
Accent Color ruby

materials Cardstock (WorldWin)
Patterned Paper (EK Success)
Stamp, Brads, Ink (Stampin' Up!)
Ribbon • Hemp

Creative Kick-Starts!

Color

Go to an antique store and search for items from the 1930's. Some things to look for might be old magazines, books, or signs.

Journaling

Read a best-selling mystery or suspense novel, then write a story incorporating your own family into the plot!

Design

Turn on your favorite Jazz CD and jot down any words that come to your mind as you listen. Use these words in your next design.

Roaring '20s

we do not remember *days*
we remember *moments*

berries
swanky
dolled up
goofy
hotsy totsy
bee's knees
cat's pajamas
nifty
ducky
spiffy
crush
ritzy

tan fancy
cinnamon stick
morning mist
sailor blue
emerald dandy

My Grandmother

Dominant Color sailor blue
Secondary Color tan fancy
Accent Color cinnamon stick
and jet black

materials Cardstock (WorldWin) • Patterned
Paper (BasicGrey, Daisy D's, Autumn Leaves, Die
Cuts With A View) • Frames (Chatterbox) • Ink
Photo Corners • Thread • Ribbon

Remember days of youth...
Sweet Innocence
Remember when the weight of the
World was light as a feather.
—CC Milam

Color It! Color Combinations

tan fancy

cinnamon stick sailor blue

emerald dandy

morning mist cinnamon stick

sailor blue

tan fancy emerald dandy

cinnamon stick

sailor blue tan fancy

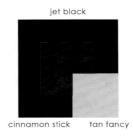

morning mist

emerald dandy sailor blue

jet black

cinnamon stick tan fancy

jet black

emerald dandy morning mist

tan fancy

sailor blue cinnamon stick

emerald dandy

sailor blue morning mist

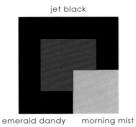

sailor blue

morning mist tan fancy

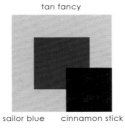

cinnamon stick

emerald dandy jet black

morning mist

cinnamon stick emerald dandy

tan fancy

emerald dandy cinnamon stick

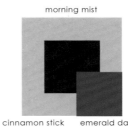

emerald dandy

tan fancy jet black

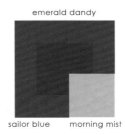

jet black

sailor blue tan fancy

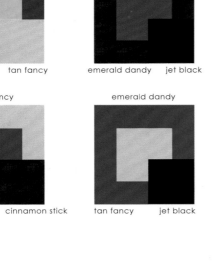

Create It!

Silent Films

Dance Marathons

Raccoon Coats

The Charleston

The Fox Trot

Bobbed Hair

Long Pearl Necklaces

It makes no difference how poor a man is; if he has a family, he's rich.

Creative Kick-Starts!

Search through old family heirlooms, jewelry, or mementos for color inspiration.

Time Travel. Imagine what your life would be like if you were living in the 1920's. Where would you live and work? What would your family be like?

Watch a silent film and take note of the unique typographic styles and designs.

Sun Valley

Dominant Color cinnamon stick
Secondary Color tan fancy
Accent Colors sailor blue and morning mist

materials Cardstock (WorldWin)
Metal Accents (Making Memories)
Ink • Ribbon

Family

Dominant Color jet black
Secondary Color cinnamon stick
Accent Colors emerald dandy and tan fancy

materials Cardstock (WorldWin, Chatterbox) • Patterned Paper (Daisy D's) • Frame (Chatterbox) Brads (Making Memories) • Letters (K&Company) • Ink • Ribbon • Thread

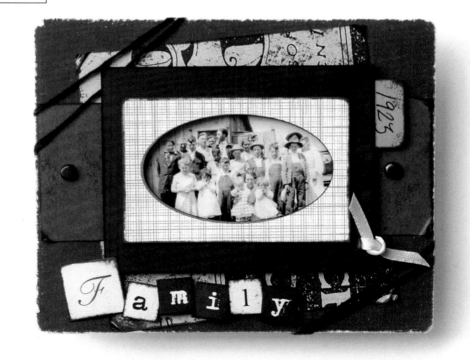

Nostalgic

we are the *hero* of our own *story*

—Mary McCarthy

slick

dashing

good egg

pert

heavens to betsy

rip-roaring

cavort

mosey along

bustle

high-falutin'

beat all

fixings

heirloom brown

gold gild

camel

mulberry

vintage olive

Paris, First World War

Dominant Color gold gild
Secondary Color mulberry
Accent Color heirloom brown

materials Cardstock (WorldWin) · Patterned
Paper (Keeping Memories Alive) · Chalk · Ribbon

The most treasured heirlooms are the sweet memories of family.

Color It! Color Combinations

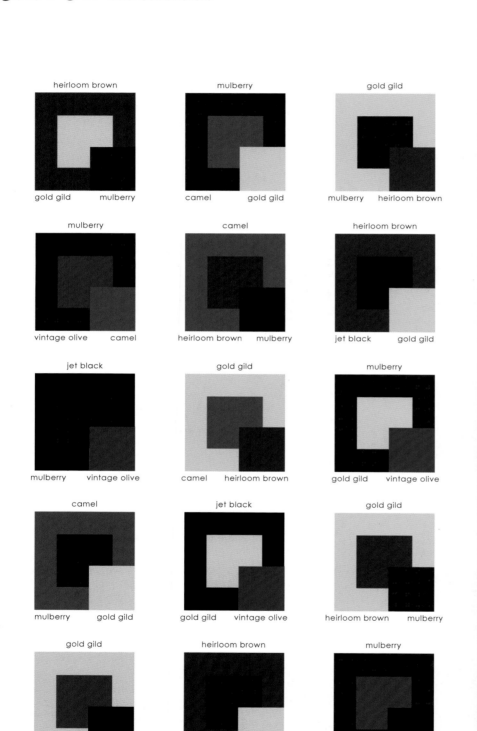

heirloom brown / gold gild / mulberry

mulberry / camel / gold gild

gold gild / mulberry / heirloom brown

mulberry / vintage olive / camel

camel / heirloom brown / mulberry

heirloom brown / jet black / gold gild

jet black / mulberry / vintage olive

gold gild / camel / heirloom brown

mulberry / gold gild / vintage olive

camel / mulberry / gold gild

jet black / gold gild / vintage olive

gold gild / heirloom brown / mulberry

gold gild / vintage olive / jet black

heirloom brown / mulberry / gold gild

mulberry / vintage olive / jet black

Create It!

Christmas

WWI

Ragtime Music

Teddy Bears

First Newsreels

Ice-Cream Cones

Phonographs

*Are you going home for Christmas?
Have you written you'll be there?
Going home to kiss the mother and
to show her that you care? Going
home to greet the father in a way to
make him glad? If you're not I hope
there'll never come a time you'll wish
you had. Just sit down and write a
letter—It will make their heartstrings
hum with a tune of perfect gladness—
If you'll tell them that you'll come.*

—Edgar A. Guest

Creative Kick-Starts!

Color

Visit a local antique shop and hunt for vintage signs and old packaging.

Journaling

Some people come into our lives and we are never the same again. Write a letter to someone who is no longer living but has touched your life in some way.

Design

Create a treasure map to something, maybe a family heirloom or homestead. Be sure to include "X marks the spot!"

Merry Christmas

Dominant Color mulberry
Secondary Color vintage olive
and heirloom brown
Accent Color white

materials Cardstock (WorldWin) • Frame, Tag (Chatterbox) • Brads (Making Memories) Ink • Chalk • Ribbon • Christmas Stamp

The Ranch

Dominant Color vintage olive
Secondary Color mulberry
Accent Color gold gild

materials Cardstock (WorldWin) • Stamps, Ink (Stampin' Up!) • Hemp • Thread

About the Author

The Family

The family is like a book—
The children are the leaves,
The parents are the covers
That protecting beauty gives.

At first the pages of the book
Are blank and purely fair,
But Time soon writeth memories
And painteth pictures there.

Love is the little golden clasp
That bindeth up the trust;
Oh, break it not, lest all the leaves
Should scatter and be lost!

—Anonymous

In writing this book, I've created a lovely scrapbook of my family. I thank them for allowing me to show you a glimpse into their personal lives. This poem was very dear to my Grandmother's heart, and her love for family tradition inspired me to begin my scrapbooking journey. I hope this book will also inspire you to preserve your family's memories!

—Misti

Misti Tracy earned a Bachelor of Fine Art degree in Graphic Design from Boise State University. She is the Creative Director of Teeter Bugs, a family-owned company which provides innovative products to scrapbookers, cardmakers, and papercrafters. She's known for her unique blending of color so it's fitting that her first book is about the wonderful world of color! She hopes it will inspire her readers to be adventurous in using color in their own creations! Living in Idaho, Misti enjoys camping and photography. She's active in her church and puts God first in her life. And, of course, she's an avid scrapbooker!

What is a Teeter Bug? It's a soft, sweet little thing, that has light-colored hair, big blue eyes and an enchanting smile! That was Misti when she was a little girl. Her Daddy stretched the last two letters of her first name into Teeter and added Bugs, because she was as cute as a bug's ear!

Michelle Johnson is a Creative Designer at Teeter Bugs. She creates exciting, new designs using the latest products and techniques! She studied music at Boise State University and she creates her designs "with a song in her heart." Michelle and her husband, Aaron, live in Idaho and enjoy camping, fishing, and being outdoors. They are the parents of a beautiful two-year-old daughter, Autumn, whose favorite saying is, "I'm not a baby. I'm a silly goose!"

Acknowledgements

I would like to thank these companies for allowing me to use their products in the making of my scrapbook pages, cards, and gifts.

I would also like to thank Michelle Johnson, Teeter Bugs' Creative Designer, for providing many of the beautiful card and scrapbook designs found throughout the book!

Most of the delightful quotes and verses were taken from Linda LaTourelle's inspiring books, "The Ultimate Guide to the Perfect Word," and "The Ultimate Guide to the Perfect Card." I want to thank her for graciously allowing me to use them! Her books can be found at

www.BluegrassPublishing.com

Arctic Frog (www.arcticfrog.net) *pages* 16, 84, 86

Autumn Leaves (www.autumnleaves.com) *pages* 62, 108, 144

BasicGrey (www.basicgrey.com) *pages* 52, 104, 128, 130, 134, 136, 138, 144

Carolee's Creations (www.ccpaper.com) *page* 22

Chatterbox (www.chatterboxinc.com) *pages* 18, 24, 26, 28, 30, 36, 42, 44, 48, 52, 62, 70, 82, 88, 90, 100, 102, 106, 108, 112, 114, 120, 126, 128, 130, 134, 136, 144, 146, 150

Colors By Design (www.colorsbydesign.com) *page* 92

Creative Impressions (www.creativeimpressions.com) *pages* 20, 38, 80, 116, 136

Creative Imaginations (www.cigift.com) *pages* 32, 34, 46, 60, 96, 114

Daisy D's (www.daisyds.com) *pages* 44, 50, 66, 134, 144, 146

EK Success (www.eksuccess.com) *page* 142

Frances Meyer (www.francesmeyer.com) *pages* 32, 34, 44, 56, 58

Die Cuts With A View (www.dcwv.com) *pages* 12, 14, 24, 28, 36, 38, 40, 46, 48, 56, 58, 60, 66, 72, 74, 78, 82, 84, 86, 88, 96, 98, 100, 112, 116, 118, 130, 138, 144

Junkitz (www.junkitz.com) *pages* 20, 22, 26

K&Company (www.kandcompany.com) *pages* 18, 130, 132, 134, 142, 146

Karen Foster (www.karenfosterdesigns.com) *page* 114

Keeping Memories Alive (www.scrapbooks.com) *pages* 112, 120, 122, 128, 148

Lasting Impressions (www.lastingimpressions.com) *page* 140

MM's Designs (www.mmsdesigns.com) *page* 38

Making Memories (www.makingmemories.com) *pages* 12, 16, 18, 26, 28, 32, 36, 38, 42, 52, 54, 62, 64, 66, 68, 74, 78, 94, 96, 100, 102, 104, 112, 114, 122, 126, 130, 134, 142, 146, 150

me and my BIG ideas (www.meandmybigideas.com) *pages* 132, 138, 140

NRN Designs (www.nrndesigns.com) *pages* 34, 46, 66, 76

Paper Adventures (www.paperadventures.com) *page* 80

Prima Marketing (www.mulberrypaperflowers.com) *pages* 34, 48, 50

Prismacolor (www.prismacolor.com) *page* 52

Scrapworks (www.scrapworks.com) *page* 20

Stampin' Up! (www.stampinup.com) *pages* 18, 22, 42, 46, 48, 51, 52, 58, 62, 68, 70, 72, 78, 82, 86, 88, 90, 94, 98, 100, 106, 110, 120, 122, 124, 130, 134, 142, 150

Sullivans (www.sullivans.net) *pages* 62, 94, 128, 130, 132, 136

Tsukineko (www.tsukineko.com) *pages* 22, 62, 70, 74, 78, 104, 106, 114

Two Busy Moms *pages* 40, 42, 142

WorldWin Papers (www.worldwinpapers.com) *pages* 12, 14, 18, 22, 28, 30, 32, 34, 42, 44, 46, 52, 54, 56, 58, 60, 64, 68, 70, 76, 82, 88, 92, 94, 96, 98, 100, 102, 104, 106, 108, 110, 112, 114, 116, 118, 120, 122, 124, 126, 128, 130, 132, 134, 136, 138, 140, 142, 144, 146, 148, 150

Thank You!

Other Books Available
from Bluegrass Publishing

Best Sellers

The Ultimate Guide to the Perfect Word
(Bluegrass Publishing's biggest seller—over 200,000 copies sold!)
Linda LaTourelle

The Ultimate Guide to the Perfect Card
(The largest collection of sentiments and sayings for the creative cardmaker!)
Linda LaTourelle

The Ultimate Guide to Celebrating Kids I
(Birth through preschool—384 pages)
Linda LaTourelle

The Ultimate Guide to Celebrating Kids II
(All New—Grade School—384 pages)
Linda LaTourelle

LoveLines
(Book 1 in the series "Perfect Words Worth Repeating")
(Artistic quotes to be used time and again)
Linda LaTourelle

Where's Thena? I Need a Poem About...
(Insightful & witty poems)
Thena Smith

Whispers
(Passionate poetry & words of love)
Thena Smith

A Taste of Paste
(Poems for the classroom)
Thena Smith

BoardSmartz
(Learning quips & bulletin board tips)
Thena Smith

What Can I Say?
(Words with an artistic flair)
WendiSue

New Products Now Available

Letters to Heaven
(Words of comfort for the grieving)
Thena Smith and Lynne Carey

The Whole Megillah
(Poetry with a Jewish flair)
Carla Birnberg

Clear Quotes
(Word art with a view)
Linda LaTourelle

BritWit
(Full-color photographic word art)
Julie McGuffee

Coming Attractions

C is for Christmas
(Poetry for the season)
Thena Smith

Pocketful of Poems
(Pocket-sized poems for perfect pages)
Lisa Stiglic

A Mother's Heart—A Father's Wisdom
(Book 2 in the series "Perfect Words Worth Repeating")
Linda LaTourelle

Watch for our new line of Digital Products coming soon!

Also, be sure to watch for all of the Ultimate line
of products on Shop at Home TV!

More Surprises Coming Soon!

Bluegrass Publishing proudly sponsors the *National Scrapbook Association* database. Serving all segments of the scrapbooking industry, the NSA provides the tools to strengthen and unify the scrapbooking community and is dedicated to *expanding the passion* of scrapbooking. See www.nsa.gs for more information.

It Couldn't Be Easier!

ORDER FORM

Name: _____   Date: _____

Address: _____   City/St/Zip: _____

E-mail: _____   Phone: (_____) _____ - _____

PAYMENT INFORMATION

Check: (#_____) **Credit Card:** ☐ Visa ☐ MasterCard ☐ Discover ☐ American Express

Credit Card Number _____ 3 Digit Security Code _____

Expiration Date _____ Name (as shown on card) _____

☐ Please send me "The Ultimate Line" newsletter and promotional offers as they become available.

TOTAL $_____

DESCRIPTION	QTY	UNIT	TOTAL
Ultimate Guide to the Perfect Word		19.95	
Ultimate Card - 2nd Edition		19.95	
Ultimate Kids I (Birth-Preschool)		19.95	
Ultimate Kids II (K-6th Grade)		19.95	
LoveLines		12.95	
Where's Thena? I need a poem about...		19.95	
Whispers		12.95	
What Can I Say?		12.95	
BoardSmartz		14.95	
Taste of Paste		14.95	
Clear Quotes—Autumn		2.25	
Clear Quotes—Baby Month by Month		2.25	
Clear Quotes—Christmas		2.25	
Clear Quotes—LoveLines		2.25	
Clear Quotes—Military		2.25	
Clear Quotes—Pets		2.25	
Clear Quotes—School Days		2.25	
Column One Total			

DESCRIPTION	QTY	UNIT	TOTAL
Letters to Heaven		14.95	
BW—Borders - Seasons of the Year		3.50	
BW—Borders - Garden Party		3.50	
BW—Borders - April Showers		3.50	
BW—Borders - Sunset Serenade		3.50	
BW—Borders - Treasures Deep		3.50	
The Whole Megillah (Scrapbooking Jewish)		12.95	
Color Made Easy - Color Palette *NEW		24.95	
Pocketful of Poems—Babies Vol 1		7.95	
Pocketful of Poems—Toddlers Vol 2		7.95	
Pocketful of Poems—Kids Inc. Vol 3		7.95	
Pocketful of Poems—Teen Thing Vol 4		7.95	
C is for Christmas		17.95	

*Shipping $2.95 for the first item and $1.00 each additional Book or CD

Total This Column	$
Total Column One	$
Kentucky 6% Tax (if applicable)	$
Shipping	$
TOTAL ORDER	$

Call for quote on custom or priority shipping

Ship To (if different than billing address):

NAME:	
ADDRESS:	
CITY/STATE/ZIP:	
PHONE:	CONTACT:

BP

Bluegrass Publishing, Inc.
PO Box 634 • Mayfield, KY 42066
(270) 251-3600 • Fax (270) 251-3603
www.BluegrassPublishing.com
E-mail: service@theultimateword.com

cut along dotted line

Thank You!
for your order

www.theultimateword.com
270·251·3600

Color Buddy ™

The *Color Buddy*™ is an invaluable tool. It's compact and portable. It can go with you anywhere to make choosing paper and embellishments faster and easier!

Color Buddy™, Teeter Bugs ©2006

INSTRUCTIONS... Remove color palettes along perforated lines. Punch a hole in the end of each palette and insert a metal ring, which can be purchased at office supply stores.

jet black

white

vanilla bean

morning mist

decadence

neutral

Color Buddy ™
Teeter Bugs ™

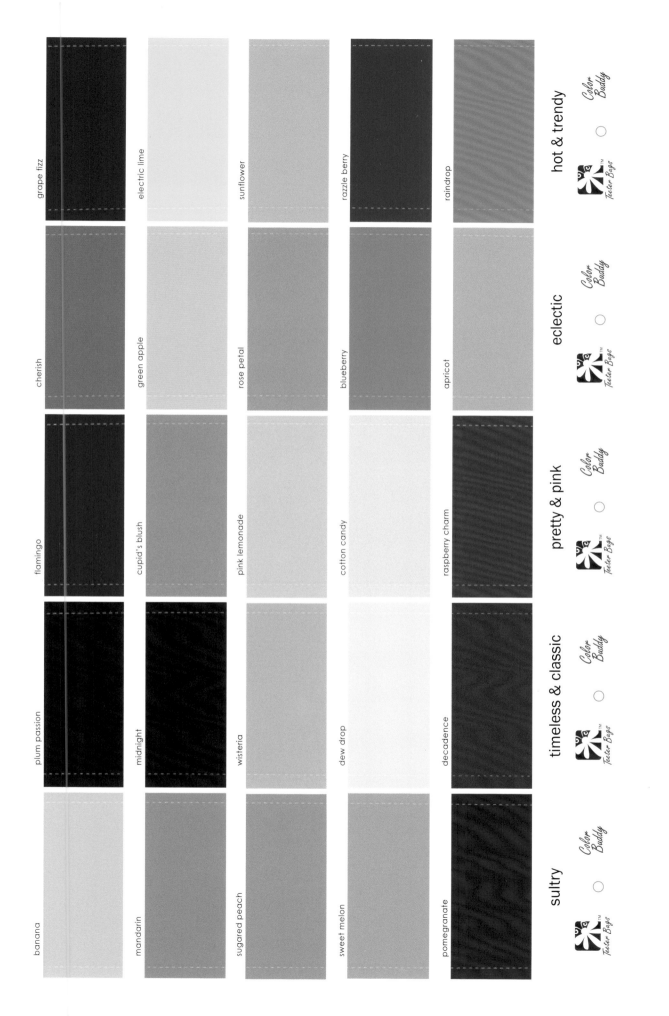

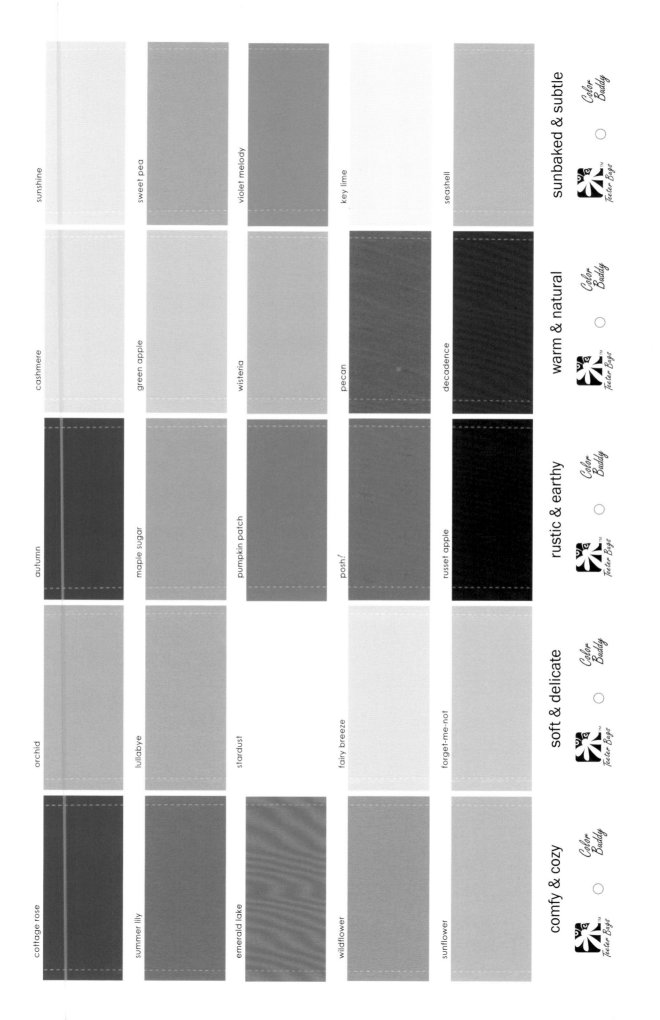

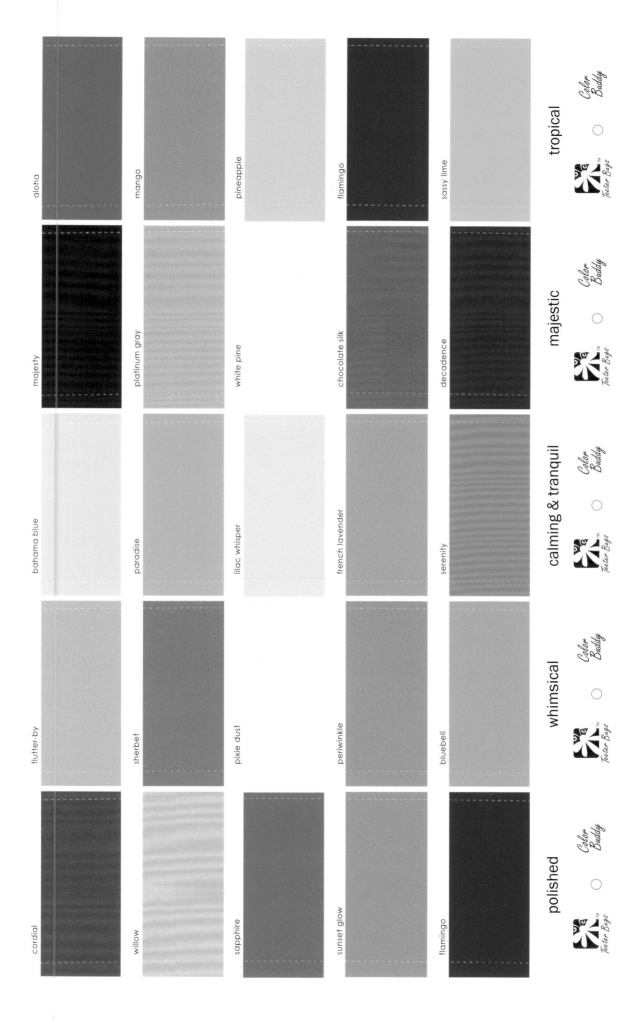

polished

whimsical

calming & tranquil

majestic

tropical

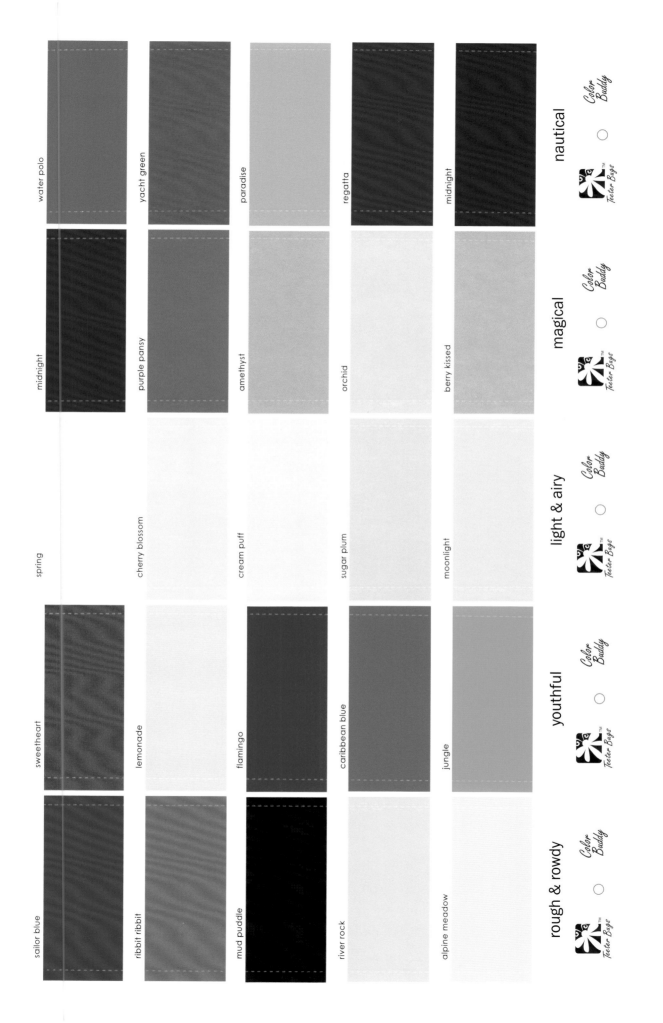

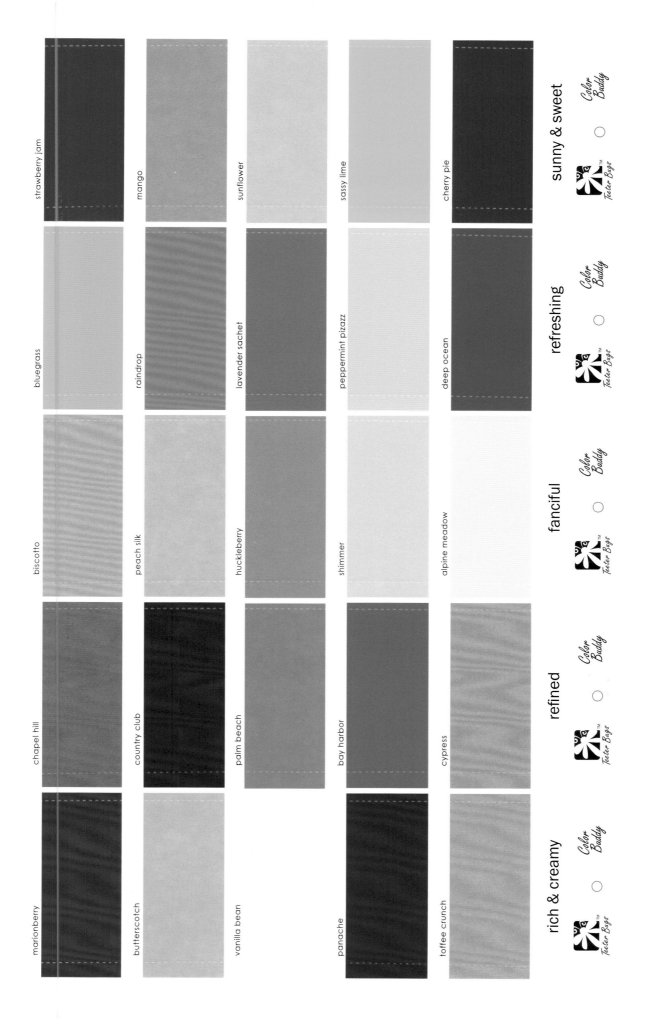

strawberry jam

mango

sunflower

sassy lime

cherry pie

sunny & sweet

Color Buddy

Teeter Bugs™

bluegrass

raindrop

lavender sachet

peppermint pizazz

deep ocean

refreshing

Color Buddy

Teeter Bugs™

biscotto

peach silk

huckleberry

shimmer

alpine meadow

fanciful

Color Buddy

Teeter Bugs™

chapel hill

country club

palm beach

bay harbor

cypress

refined

Color Buddy

Teeter Bugs™

marionberry

butterscotch

vanilla bean

panache

toffee crunch

rich & creamy

Color Buddy

Teeter Bugs™

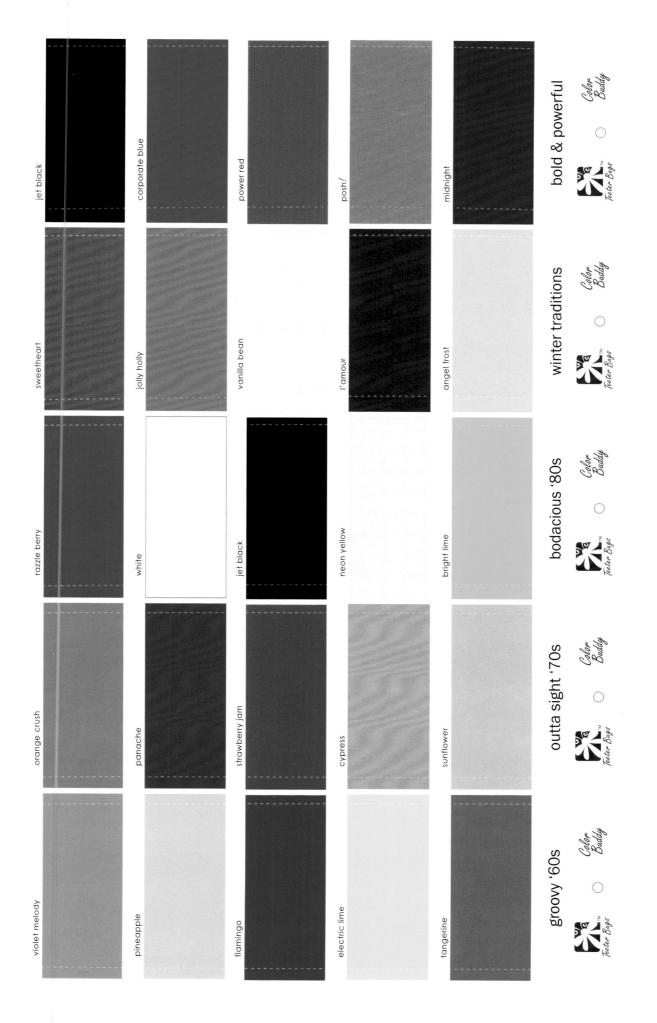